D1608659

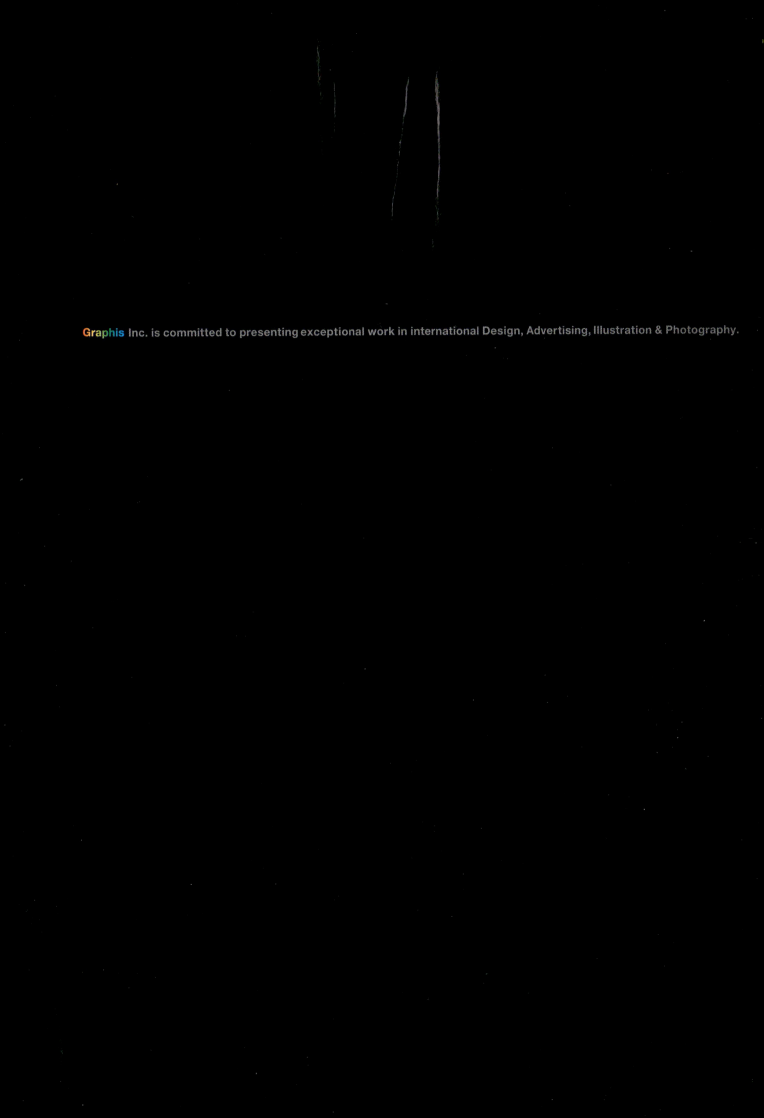

Graphis Inc. is committed to presenting exceptional work in international Design, Advertising, Illustration & Photography.

Published by **Graphis** | Publisher & Creative Director: B. Martin Pedersen | Design: Yon Joo Choi and Gregory Michael Cerrato | Editorial: Abigail Newman-Lapp | Production: Jennifer R. Berlingeri and Abigail Newman-Lapp | Webmaster: Abigail Newman-Lapp | Support Staff: Rita Jones Design & Production Interns: Kristen Marie Rego and Caryn Tsai | Editorial Interns: Amy L. Bergen, Kendra Cunningham and Bridget Marie Hill

Remarks: We extend our heartfelt thanks to contributors throughout the world who have made it possible to publish a wide and international spectrum of the best work in this field. Entry instructions for all Graphis Books may be requested from: Graphis Inc., 307 Fifth Avenue, Tenth Floor, New York, New York 10016, or visit our web site at www.graphis.com.

Anmerkungen: Unser Dank gilt den Einsendern aus aller Welt, die es uns ermöglicht haben, ein breites, internationales Spektrum der besten Arbeiten zu veröffentlichen. Teilnahmebedingungen für die Graphis-Bücher sind erhältlich bei: Graphis, Inc., 307 Fifth Avenue, Tenth Floor, New York, New York 10016. Besuchen Sie uns im World Wide Web, www.graphis.com.

Remerciements: Nous remercions les participants du monde entier qui ont rendu possible la publication de cet ouvrage offrant un panorama complet des meilleurs travaux. Les modalités d'inscription peuvent être obtenues auprès de: Graphis, Inc., 307 Fifth Avenue, Tenth Floor, New York, New York 10016. Rendez-nous visite sur notre site web: www.graphis.com.

Contents

InMemoriam

John Henry Alvin
*Movie Poster Illustrator,
Cinematic Artist & Painter*
1948~2008

Les Barton
Cartoonist & Illustrator
1923~2008

Edd Cartier
Science Fiction Illustrator
1914~2008

Lou Dorfsman
Designer, Design Chief at CBS
1918~2008

Shigeo Fukuda
Graphic Designer
1932~2009

Miroslav Havel
Glass Designer
1922~2008

Jan Kaplický
Architect
1937~2009

Ted Lapidus
Clothing Designer
1929~2008

Yves Saint Laurent
Fashion Designer
1936~2008

Oliver Lincoln Lundquist
Architect & Industrial Designer
1916~2008

Pierre Mendell
Graphic Designer
1916~2008

Jørn Utzon
Architect
1929~2008

Sylvia Wishart
Painter & Illustrator
1936~2008

Andrew Wyeth
Painter
1917~2009

Das Einfache einfach einfach zu gestalten, war Pierre Mendells große Leidenschaft.
To create symplicity simply simple was Pierre's great passion in life.

Uwe Loesch

My first reaction was he was good 'till the end and for me this is a great homage. Pierre Mendell was not young anymore, but his work was still current among the best in the industry. Time is cruel. The honor an artist receives in the last stages of life generally recalls past glorious periods, but these honors cannot hide that the artist is not anymore a talented creator. This was not the case of Pierre Mendell. His poster design work remained classic, powerful, intelligent, and out of fashion until the end.

Alain Le Quernec

In the flow of pictures only a few will be noticed and the best will be remembered.

Kari Piippo

We have lost a remarkable man. Pierre was a great designer, simply one of the best. I always admired his posters; clear idea, clear message, clear typography, a clear and convincing humor... that is poster art!

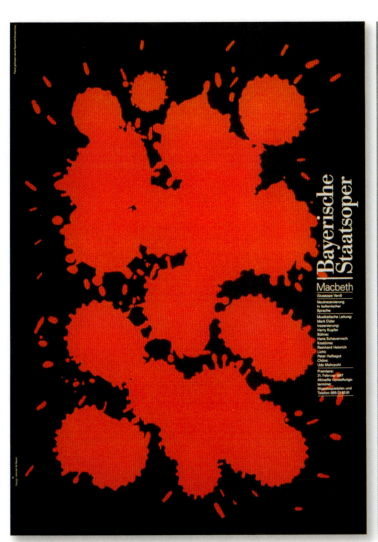

Professor Günter Rambow: Pierre Mendell's Eulogy

My first encounter with Pierre was at the International Advertising and Art magazine 'Gebrauchsgraphik' in 1968. Two young and excellent design teams had been featured—Mendell and Oberer as well as Rambow and Lienemeyer. Mendell and Oberer's design was clean and minimal, with a preference towards rational solutions. Having said that, there was an anarchic element in each of their presented works. i.e. for BOLS—a peach stuck on the handle of a cognac glass captured in the style of photo realism with the BOLS logo below. Absolute minimal you couldn't reduce it any more.

This minimalism was very exciting, thrilling and even to a degree scandalous, all by using a kind of formal and rational language. In describing this earlier design, I have also described an important aspect of your personality.

With rational language, related to Type and Image, you challenged the usual habits of perception and viewing. This gave your messages such power. It was impossible to escape the design and this effect was the key to your posters, which made you one of the great poster designers of the century.

Your work is in all the important poster collections throughout the world—archived, exhibited and publicized. In 2006, I myself had the opportunity to handle and analyze your posters for the poster exhibition in my gallery titled 'Posters by Pierre Mendell,' showing your posters from the 60s to the more recent designs.

While handling and organizing the various posters, I experienced a personal connection and, somehow, a kind of dialogue between your designs and myself. I looked at your work in admiration and saw you as an older brother.

Your Corporate Identity work for both internationally known companies, as well as for small and medium sized companies, also shows sensitivity. Your designs were cultured and humanistic, never a slave to order like some German design companies, far away from Otl Aichers dogmatic rules. For VITRA, you created a typographical 'cosmos' under which products and personalities such as Carles and Ray Eames, Le Corbusier, Gerrit Rietveld, Mies van der Rohe, Marcel Breuer, Mart Stam just to name a few representatives of modern design.

You also created some fantastic packaging, brochures and catalogues etc. for an international metal manufacturing and toolmaking company. All your identity designs reflected the enthusiastic entrepreneurism of the individual companies and their products. These various identities reflected partly also your own personality. You had a special cultured aura, always an exquisite taste, well dressed—the material was simple and of high quality. You always had a friendly expression on your face with a curious twinkle in your eyes. Your smile was experienced as a source of warm friendliness by everybody I know.

In your spacious atelier along the river Isar, in Munich, there was always a big bunch of white Lillies in a white porcelain vase. The style of your office interior was of classical modernity, tasteful and of good quality. 2-3 recent pieces of work were framed and usually leaning against the walls. During the last years I noticed a framed poster above your desk. It showed a black man dressed in a suit, white shirt and black tie. His head was in monochrome green color. The title was: 'Everybody is equal before God.'

Pierre, I know since our joint visit to Paris in the mid 80s, that you did not always experience equality from people and society. I remember a situation where we strolled along the Seine one evening. It was the Anniversary of the occupation by the fascist army. Old historical cars, bicycles, horse and carts and similar vehicles lined up along the Seine and stimulated the Parisian citizens fleeing the city towards the south part of France. All displays were to actual size and in great detail. On top of one of the bridges was a 20 m high loudspeaker erected from which you could hear a hateful propagada speech by Adolf Hitler, his hard and harsh voice in german-austrian staccato. And then you could also hear the speeches of Charles de Gaulle, Winston Churchill and Franklin D. Roosevelt.

Pierre, I remember as if it had been yesterday, when you said: 'It was exactly here where I stood in my little thin coat, the yellow star of David sewn to the collar of my coat'. For a moment I grabbed your hand and it felt like holding a trembling little boy. 10 m further on and you were again the distinguished, cultivated and friendly Pierre Mendell. I also saw your American passport at one of the border controls. Those two little moments signaled to me that your road to the guaranteed human rights must have been thorny, thin, twisted and full of danger. But then you started as a designer and created your own world. Here you operated successfully and took heed of the message in one of your designs, 'Everybody is equal before God.'

This justice is now given to you.

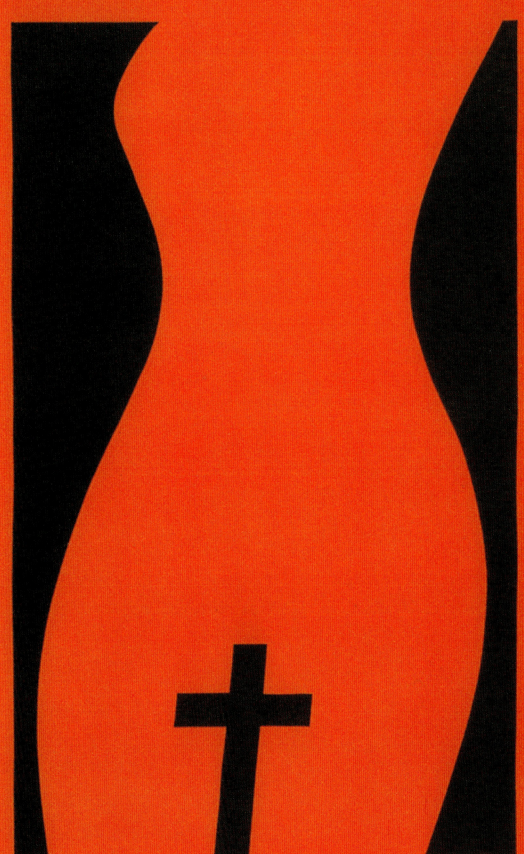

Bayerische Staatsoper

Don
Giovanni

Wolfgang Amadeus
Mozart

Neuinszenierung
In italienischer
Sprache

Musikalische Leitung:
Sir Colin Davis
Inszenierung:
Nicholas Hytner
Bühne und Kostüme:
Bob Crowley
Licht: Jean Kalman

31. Oktober 1994
(Premiere)
3., 5., 9., 11. und
13. November 1994
1., 4., 6., 11. und
18. März;
14. und 17. Juni
6. und 9. Juli 1995

SPD cover photographed by Jill Greenberg

Q&A with Robert Priest

Who gave you this assignment?

Emily Smith and Arem Duplessis at the Society of Publication Designers (SPD) asked me to design the whole book.

Were you given any direction by her?

No, whoever designs the book usually has carte blanche on the project.

How many past books have you done for SPD?

Four.

How did you start your thought process?

What we did on our past covers, as well as this one, was to respond to the entry, which was chosen by the jury, that we felt was the most visually exciting piece in the annual. The bear portrait, by Jill Greenberg, which was just off the press for the Los Angeles magazine, was part of a collection of photographs that she created. I knew the famous photographs of monkeys and the crying children that she had shot, and this shot of the bear was just such a startling image. We thought we'd use it as a platform to create the cover. What we've done in the past was to take the image that's been chosen and manipulate it, with the photographer's permission, to become the cover of SPD. In this case, we had the idea of imagining the bear having eaten something and then use the bones to form the SPD letters.

A smart direction, and the reader will know who was eaten by looking at the back cover.

Right, exactly. It was a bit of a struggle to decide whether we would leave a human skull in there or not. There was the taste issue to consider and we thought if it was the back cover and reasonably understated, people would go along with it and understand the joke.

Was this your idea?

Yes. Along with my collaborator, Grace Lee, who is a brilliant designer.

Did you bring Jill into the process at all?

Of course we asked Jill's permission for the idea and to shoot the bones so that it would be a complete piece of her work. Jill had a wonderful stylist named Ethan Tobman and he spent a good deal of time looking for the bones.

These bones were enormous. I think they were from a cow. Ethan went out to Queens somewhere, I believe, and had this enormous vat of boiling water, in which he reduced what was left of the cow into bone form. It was quite a remarkable exercise in styling, one I've never heard of before. We brought these bones to the studio; Jill was there, along with Ethan and he created the SPD letters. The amount of blood—I guess it was artificial blood that we used, I was never quite sure—didn't seem enough to me, so I kept on asking them to add more blood. We came to the moment where it wasn't completely gross and where it still worked as very aggressive typography.

Were you and Jill both pleased with the results?

Yes, very excited. She did a beautiful job combining her shot of the bones with the bear shot. She's a master of Photoshop and I think it ended up being quite successful. Very startling, of course.

Who was the first person at The Society of Publication Designers to see it and were they happy?

My contact for the covers was Arem Duplessis, who is the Art Director for the New York Times Magazine. He was responsible for the book. One of his duties as a committee member of SPD was to produce the book. He was incredibly supportive through the whole process. I explained the ideas to him and he went along. He seemed very happy with it.

Has there been any increase in sales over the last year and have members complimented you on the project?

Grace and I received a lot of compliments on it, yes. I have no idea about any increase in sales. Only SPD would know that.

Well, it's a tough thing to gauge this year because of the economy. Is there anything more you feel you would like to add to this?

No, I think that's the essence of it. It was done in short order, from the idea to calling Jill and getting Ethan on board. It was one of those projects that went well from the beginning. Everybody enjoyed participating on it and we had a lot of fun with it, which often produces the best work.

You're a highly competent designer and you made it look easy.

I appreciate that very much.

Robert Priest:
42 White Street, NY, NY 10013
www.priestmedia.com

2006~Present Condé Nast Portfolio, *Design Director*
1999~2006 Priest Media Inc., *Principal*
1997~1999 Esquire, *Design Director*
1995~1997 Relaunched House & Garden, *Design Director*
1988~1995 GQ, *Creative Director*
1985~1988 US, *Design Director*
1983~1985 Newsweek, *Design Director*
1979~1983 Esquire, *Art Director*

Awards:

Winner of numerous awards for design and art direction including twenty eight Gold Awards from The Society of Publication Designers, Art Directors Club / New York, British Design and Art Direction, Canadian National Magazine Awards and AIGA.
ASME Ellie Award for Condé Nast Portfolio's Brief section.
Co-founder of American Illustration and American Photography.

Major Projects:

2004~2006 Created O At Home for Hearst Corporation
2005 Redesigned More Magazine for Meredith
2005 Redesigned Sky Magazine for Delta Airlines
2005 Created Avon Dreams for Hearst Custom Publishing
2005 Designed The Best of Reader's Digest
2004 Created Liz Claiborne Home for Hearst Custom Publishing
2004 Created Gala for Gruner+Jahr
2003~2007 Designed Hollywood Life Magazine for Movieline
2003~2007 Designed The Society of Publication Designers
   38th, 39th, 40th, and 42nd Annuals
2003 Designed restaurant identity/packaging for Lunchbox Food Co. NY
2003 Redesigned Bloomberg Personal Finance
2000 Redesigned Yahoo! Internet Life for Ziff Davis
2001 Created Baseline, an information technology magazine for
   Ziff Davis
2000 Created a series of special issues for InStyle Magazine:
   Weddings, The Look, Makeover and Entertaining.
1999 Redesigned The Oxford American, the literary magazine.

Jill Greenberg

Jill Greenberg Studio:
8570 Wilshire Boulevard, Suite 250, Beverly Hills, CA 90211
www.manipulator.com

Biography: Since the age of 10, Jill Greenberg has been staging photographs and creating characters using the mediums of drawing, painting, sculpture, film and photography. Greenberg's notable success with gallery and museum shows, book publishing, commercial and editorial photography displays her unique perspective with a clear voice that is apparent through her distinctive lighting and personally executed post production.

About the cover: Ursine was a personal series of studio bear portraits that I did and I asked Heidi Volpe at Los Angeles Times' West Magazine, a friend and a client, if she could help finance the first shoot. Her idea was to have the bears represent six California governors and, in exchange, they could run six bears in West Magazine for their partial funding of the August 2006 shoot in Calgary. When the series in West Magazine won a SPD award, I was contacted by Robert Priest to ask if they could use the image on the cover of the SPD Annual but he wanted it modified to include the letters SPD. I suggested using bones to spell out SPD. The Ursine series was displayed in Fahey Klein in Los Angeles and Clampart in New York City. Several notable celebrities such as Tom Ford and Ashton Kutcher own some of these bear portraits, including the one used on the SPD cover. I have continued my personal series of bears in my book, Bear Portraits, published by Little, Brown, which is due out in the Fall.

Office, a San Francisco-based creative studio, has been recognized around the world for its work for clients like Target and The Coca-Cola Company. They work with leading brands and emerging businesses to clarify their stories and create tangible experiences that set them apart from the competition and connect with their customers. Office recently collaborated with 826 Valencia, a nonprofit tutoring center for aspiring young writers, which runs San Francisco's only pirate supply store, to create a new identity and nearly 50 new products. All proceeds directly benefit the organization's free writing programs. 826 Valencia was founded in 2002 and named for its address in San Francisco's Mission District. When the founders learned that the space for their new nonprofit tutoring center was zoned for commercial use, they opened a pirate supply store to meet city regulations. Since then, the unconventional storefront has drawn kids into its free writing programs held in the back. The pirate store, with eye patches, parrot food and planks sold by the foot, represents what 826's programs stand for: supporting creative expression.

The solution you came up with is quite unique. How did you arrive at this direction?

We approached this assignment the same way we do any of our projects. We started with research, immersing ourselves in all things pirate, then considered the audience: pirates, of course, and the kids, volunteers, parents, teachers, and others curious about buccaneering. We had some pretty insane brainstorming sessions, resulting in tons of ideas and several different design directions, which were then edited and refined.

Was the client involved in this process?

The people at 826 are great collaborators. 826 Valencia founder and Mc-Sweeney's editor Dave Eggers was personally involved in the process.

What was your reaction when the client came to you with this assignment of creating fictional products?

We're big fans of 826 Valencia and our team actually approached them to see if we could help out in some way, whether through volunteering or providing design services. We went there to meet with the staff and discussed the possibility of going into a local school to help kids write a book. At the end of our meeting, Dave Eggers walked in and introduced himself, and casually told us he'd love any ideas to help refresh the pirate store. We jumped on it. I think he was pretty shocked when we came back several weeks later with a new identity and a bunch of product ideas.

What was the inspiration for products with names like "peg leg oil" and "glass eye drops"?

The pirate store is a wildly imaginative, inspiring, interactive experience. We tried to create an authentic, visually cohesive story around the idea of an 18th century pirate walking into a 21st century store to pick up a few things. People really aren't buying what's inside the bottles; they're buying the idea. For example, Eau de Mer cologne is water we collected from the San Francisco Bay. But it's packaged with beautiful metallic gold patterned paper in a black wooden box with a pirate "love poem" inscripted on the bottle.

What is the biggest challenge you had to overcome with this assignment?

Once you start coming with ideas for pirate products, it's tough to stop.

What were the client's reactions on seeing the finished products?

The folks at 826 were really excited about the new identity and products. Most important, the products are helping raise money for 826 programs. After the new posters became available, online sales quintupled.

Was this project a pro-bono effort?

Yes. We consider supporting our community part of Office's purpose.

What are some other products offered?

Captain Blackbeard's Beard Extensions – Patchy spots got ya down? Fear not, Capt. Blackbeard grows 'em where you can't. So silky the ladies will swoon. So coarse your crew will covet. Recent studies have found that CBBEs are indistinguishable by 9 out of 10 naked eyes, and able to weather the most savage of gales, tidal waves, and tugs of fraternal greetings. Warning: CBBE may cause an overwhelming sense of adequacy. Captain Blackbeard's Beard Dye – Color: Black. Beards can get bleached by the sun. Beards can turn white from fear. In either case, Blackbeard's Beard Dye imparts a midnight hue to your whiskers, leaving them shiny, conditioned and bristling with health. Next time you take it on the chin, be sure it's covered with a beard you can be proud of ... a Blackbeard beard. Also suitable for mustaches and mole hair. Made for the trade; available to all.

Quick Acting Scurvy BeGone – Dosage: a tablet a day, maybe more. Each capsule contains the power of one entire lime or lemon or small lemon. Fairly probable side effects: hirsutism; supernumerary organs; chimerism; sudden onset of fake English accent; boils

Project Credits – Creative directors: Jason Schulte and Jill Robertson; Designers: Rob Alexander, Will Ecke, Gaelyn Mangrum, Jason Schulte, Jeff Bucholtz; Writers: Dave Eggers, Jon Adams, Dan Weiss, Jennifer Traig, Anna Ura, Lisa Pemrick, Ben Acker, Rob Alexander; Project manager: Elinor Hutton; Product Photography: Vanessa Chu; Headshot Photography: Jason Madara

Office: hello@visitoffice.com / www.visitoffice.com
826 Valencia Pirate Supply Store: www.826valencia.org/store

Jason Schulte, founder & creative director: Since founding Office in 2003, Jason has created differentiated work for leading brands like adidas Golf, Apple, Coca-Cola, hp, Levi's and Target. Before forming the studio, he was an art director at Goodby, Silverstein & Partners and design director at TBWA\Chiat\Day San Francisco. He started his career at the Charles S. Anderson Design Company in Minneapolis. Over the years, Jason's work has been recognized by nearly every major graphic design competition and publication, and has appeared in several books and museum exhibitions. In 2000, Print magazine named him one of the country's top 20 visual artists under age 30, and in 2007, Fast Company featured Jason as one of 14 "designers to watch" in its Masters of Design issue. He has been a speaker and judge for design organizations, and is a Directed Study Advisor at the San Francisco Academy of Art. He grew up in Green Mountain, Iowa (where there's no actual mountain) and is a graduate of Iowa State University's College of Design. Jason lives in San Francisco with his wife (and Office president) Jill Robertson and their foster dog Elvis.

Jill Robertson, president: As an 8-year-old, Jill regularly played a game she called "Office"—an imaginary creative agency (sort of) where she believed her stories and drawings of flowers, rainbows and dogs made people happy. A few years later, she's still passionate about storytelling as she manages the studio and leads projects for clients such as The Coca-Cola Company, Disney, eBay and 826 Valencia. Before joining Office, Jill worked at Gap Inc. as the communications director and speechwriter for the company's CEO. In 2007, she was among a select group of creative executives chosen to participate in the Harvard Business School and AIGA program Business Perspectives for Creative Leaders. Jill holds a J.D. from the University of Minnesota Law School and B.A. in journalism from Iowa State University, where she met her husband (and Office creative director) Jason Schulte. She's originally from Audubon, Iowa, home to Albert, the world's largest bull. Outside Office, Jill designs jewelry and aspires to write a book someday. She still likes flowers, rainbows and dogs.

BILGE WATER
from the
ATLANTIC OCEAN

BILGE WATER
from the
PACIFIC OCEAN

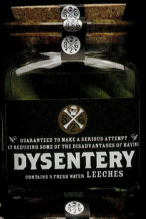

MADE FOR
the
TRADE
AVAILABLE
to ALL

FAST
ACTING
SEA
SICKNESS
TABLETS

GUARANTEED TO MAKE A SERIOUS ATTEMPT
AT REDUCING SOME OF THE DISADVANTAGES OF HAVING
DYSENTERY
CONTAINS 5 FRESH WATER LEECHES

GUARANTEED
TO RID YOU OF
THE
ITCH

GUARANTEED TO TRY VERY HARD TO RELIEVE
YOU OF THE MORE NOTICEABLE ASPECTS OF
GANGRENE
CONTAINS 5 FRESH WATER LEECHES

DECENT
PEG
LEG
OIL

826 VALENCIA

BLACKBEARD'S
EXTENSIONS.

PATCHY SPOTS GOT YA DOWN?

FEAR NOT.
CAPT. BLACKBEARD GROWS 'EM WHERE YOU CAN'T.

So silky the ladies will swoon.
So coarse your crew will covet.

Gold
TOOTH

MADE FOR
the
TRADE
AVAILABLE
to ALL

Hewlett-Packard and fashion designer Vivienne Tam joined together to become the go-to technology brand for fashionistas by creating a truly haute computer. When Vivienne Tam showed her 2009 Spring and Summer collection during the New York Fall 2009 Fashion Week, we saw the ultimate expression of digital couture. Vivienne's premier model walked down the catwalk carrying the world's first digital clutch, the ultimate manifestation of fashion meets technology.

What was the problem given when beginning this assignment?
HP wanted to connect with the modern woman. She has children, a career and takes pride in how she presents herself. She's fashion-conscious. HP wanted innovative ideas on how to connect with this target audience. We saw fashion as our "in" and wanted to connect them to that world in a bold way. We wanted to introduce fashion to technology.

How did you decide to connect with Vivienne Tam, who designed the dress and the laptop?
HP is an international brand and we knew we needed someone with international appeal. Vivienne Tam became a household name in American fashion in the mid-90s and remains wildly successful in markets all over the world, including China and fashion-forward Japan. We also knew we needed someone who created her own textiles and had a unique visual point of view. Vivienne's bold take on historic Chinese patterns with a modern-day approach further solidified the partnership as a perfect fit. We came to her with the idea, and she was almost instantly onboard. Right away, she seemed to be able to see the bigger picture.

Why was Vivienne Tam selected over other fashion designers?
Out of all the designers, she was unique not only because she creates her own patterns and textiles, but also because she instantly saw what we were trying to achieve, the idea of fashion meeting technology. She also had a distinctive point of view on the subject.

How much influence did Vivienne Tam have on the campaign?
Vivienne's designs influenced the visual style of the campaign. She wanted to create an organic feel, which she achieved by using graphic florals throughout the marketing campaign. She also spent time with the creative team and approved every creative piece that was presented.

Why were peonies selected as such a large part of her design?
In many ways, peonies represent the facets of what Vivienne was trying to achieve with the laptop design, with fashion meeting technology. Inherently, they are true to Vivienne's design aesthetic and are commonly used forms in Chinese art. However, Vivienne saw deeper meaning when the flower design was placed on the computer, as it transformed the computer, which is typically a cold, standardized item, into a personalized piece of art. It was this point of view that tied directly into HP's brand philosophy, "The computer is personal again." Women keep their whole lives on their computers, so she reflected that in a tranquil, elegant, fashion-forward way.

Was the dress designed to match the laptop or the laptop designed to match the dress?
The collection was thought out holistically. There was no distinction between the notebook and the clothing. The idea of a woman being "layered" worked directly into both areas of the collection.

Are additional colors and designs of the laptop available?
While there were no additional external variations of color for the mini, Vivienne worked with us to help design different customizable icons, wallpapers and screen savers for the inside of the HP Mini Vivienne Tam Edition.

How was the laptop received by the public after Tam's fashion show during New York's Fall 2009 Fashion Week?
The laptop was a huge hit. After the show, everyone was asking where could they buy one "right now." At the after party, all the guests eyeing the mini in the glass case—the centerpiece of the party—had the same reaction: "I want that, now."

How was the campaign received by the client?
The client loved the campaign. It ended up being a very harmonious working relationship. We did forward-thinking online creative, ranging from a designer tour around the fashion world guided by Vivienne Tam herself to a virtual catwalk that allowed the user to strut their stuff in Vivienne's latest designs on the runway. We even offered a downloadable widget packet with Vivienne Tam desktop accessories, including desktop icons, wallpaper, and screensaver. We did timely and well-placed print; and above all, just the buzz surrounding a computer coming down the runway during the Fall 2009 New York Fashion Week made HP a very happy client.

Has the client seen an increase in attention or sales, especially with the female demographic, since the release of the laptop in December 2008?
The PR response has been overwhelming, with over 100,000,000+ media/PR-based online impressions. There have been over 900 articles published worldwide announcing the product, with editorial exposure in top fashion magazines including Elle, Vogue, and Vanity Fair, and leading global newspapers such as New York Times, International Herald Tribune, Financial Times. Network television show Desperate Housewives featured the product in an episode this spring, and Rachel Ray included a short expose piece on the product in one of her shows this winter. In terms of actual product sales, the Asia-Pacific region has already sold out of the product, and Tokyo doubled their demand after selling out of their entire volume in just ten business days.

List of Retailers Carrying the Product:
hpdirect.com, Best Buy, Confederacy (LA), Neiman Marcus, Macy's, Harrod's, Amazon.com, Vivienne Tam Boutiques WorldWide including Tokyo, Beijing, Thailand, Singapore, Hong Kong and New York

Project Credit – Account Directors: Martha Jurzynski, Nancy Reyes; Account Manager: Julia Gilbert; Art Director: Tanner Shea; Assistant Account Manager: Katie Temple; Consumer Notebook Director of ID: Stacy Wolff; Consumer Notebook Marketing: Betsy Cluck; Creative Director, Partner: Steve Simpson; Designer: Vivienne Tam; Director, Global Marketing: Tracey Trachta; Global Initiatives: Kerry Chrapliwy; Global Marketing Director: Alan Wang; Group Creative Directors, Associate Partners: Rick Condos, Hunter Hindman; Senior Vice President, Global Marketing: Satjiv Chahil; Vice President, Global Marketing: David Roman; Writer: Michelle Hirschberg

Goodby, Silverstein & Partners:
720 California Street, San Francisco, CA 94108, United States
Tel 415 955 5683 / www.goodbysilverstein.com

Goodby, Silverstein & Partners: Goodby, Silverstein & Partners is a full-service advertising agency, founded in 1983, with the simple aim of producing the world's best advertising (as recognized by its industry peers in terms of the distinctiveness of its work and by its effectiveness in the marketplace). Located in San Francisco, GS&P handles over two billion dollars in billings for clients including Hewlett-Packard, Comcast, Sprint, Adobe, Propel, Nintendo, Haagen-Dazs, Elizabeth Arden, Frito-Lay, and the California Fluid Milk Processors Advisory Board ("got milk?").

Certainly GS&P would be on almost anyone's list of the top creative agencies in the country, most often at or near the top. They have won every major advertising award, most of them many times over. GS&P has won eighteen Gold Effie™ awards from the American Marketing Association. They have had more finalists in the Kelly Awards for magazine advertising than any agency in the country. They have won Emmys, Grand Prix at Cannes, and numerous Agency of the Year awards from the Clios, Graphis, One Club, M&Ms, *AdWeek*, *AdAge*, *Creativity* and *Campaign* magazines.

The PR response has been overwhelming, with over 100,000,000 online impressions as well as over 900 articles published worldwide announcing the product.

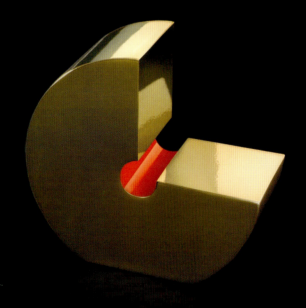

Graphis Platinum & Gold Award Winners by Location

The Americas

North America:

Canada	013
United States	130

American Island Areas:

American Samoa	000
Guam	000
Mexico	000
Northern Marianis	000
Palau	000
Puerto Rico	000
Virgin Islands	000

Caribbean:

Antigua and Barbuda	000
Bahamas	000
Barbados	000
Cayman Island	000
Cuba	000
Dominica	000
Dominican Republic	000
Grenada	000
Haiti	000
Jamaica	000
St. Kitts and Nevis	000
St. Lucia	000
St. Vincent&The Grenadines	000
Trinidad&Tobago	000

Central America:

Belize	000
Costa Rica	000
El Salvador	000
Guatemala	000
Honduras	000
Nicaragua	000
Panama	000

South America:

Argentina	000
Bolivia	000
Brazil	000
Chile	000
Colombia	000
Ecuador	000
Guyana	000
Paraguay	000
Peru	000
Uruguay	000
Venezuela	000

Europe&Africa

Europe:

Northern Europe

Aland	000
Denmark	001
Faroe Islands	000
Finland	000
Greenland	000
Iceland	000
Karelia	000
Kola Peninsula	000
Norway	004
Sweden	001
Svalbard	000

Eathern Europe

Czech Republic	000
Hungary	000
Poland	000
Romania	000
Slovak Republic	000

Baltic States

Estonia	000
Latvia	000
Lithuania	000

Western Europe

Austria	000
Belgium	000
France	000
Germany	004
Ireland	000
Italy	003
Netherlands	003
Portugal	000
Spain	003
Switzerland	000
UK	006

Commonwealth of Independent States

Armenia	000
Azerbaijan	000
Belarus	000
Georgia	000
Kazaskstan	000
Kyrgyzstan	000
Moldova	000
Russian Federation	001
Tajikistan	000
Turkmenistan	000
Ukraine	000
Uzbekistan	000

Southeast Europe

Albania	000
Bosnia-Herzegovina	000
Bulgaria	000
Croatia	003
Cyprus	000
Greece	000
Macedonia	000
Malta	000
Serbia&Montenegro	000
Slovenia	001
Turkey	000

Middle East:

Bahrain	000
Iran	000
Iraq	000
Israel / Occupied Territories	001
Jordan	000
Kuwait	000
Lebanon	000
Palestinian Authority	000
Saudi Arabia	000
Syria	000
UAE	000
Yemen	000

Africa:

North Africa

Algeria	000
Egypt	000
Libya	000
Morocco West Sahara	000
Tunisia	000

Central Africa

Burundi	000
Cameroon	000
Cent. African Rep.	000
Chad	000
Congo	000
DR Congo	000
Equatorial Guinea	000
Rwanda	000

Southern Africa

Angola	000
Malawi	000
Mozambique	000
Namibia	000
South Africa	000
Swaziland	000
Zambia	000
Zimbabwe	000

East Africa

Eritrea	000
Ethiopia	000
Kenya	000
Somalia	000
Sudan	000
Tanzania	000
Uganda	000

West Africa

Burkina Faso	000
Cote D'ivoire	000
Ghana	000
Guinea	000
Guinea-Bissau	000
Liberia	000
Mauritania	000
Niger	000
Nigeria	000
Senegal	000
Sierra Leone	000
Togo	000

Asia&Oceania

Asia:

East Asia

China	002
Japan	003
Mongolia	000
North Korea	000
South Korea	001
Taiwan	001

Southwest Asia

Brunei Darussalam	000
Cambodia	000
Indonesia	000
Laos	000
Malaysia	000
Myanmar	000
Philippines	000
Singapore	001
Thailand	000
Timor-Leste	000
Viet Nam	000

South Asia

Afghanistan	000
Bangladesh	000
Bhutan	000
India	000
Maldives	000
Nepal	000
Pakistan	000
Sri Lanka	000

Oceania:

Australia	010
Fiji	000
New Zealand	013
Papua New Guinea	000
Solomon Islands	000

Total Winning Entries **205**

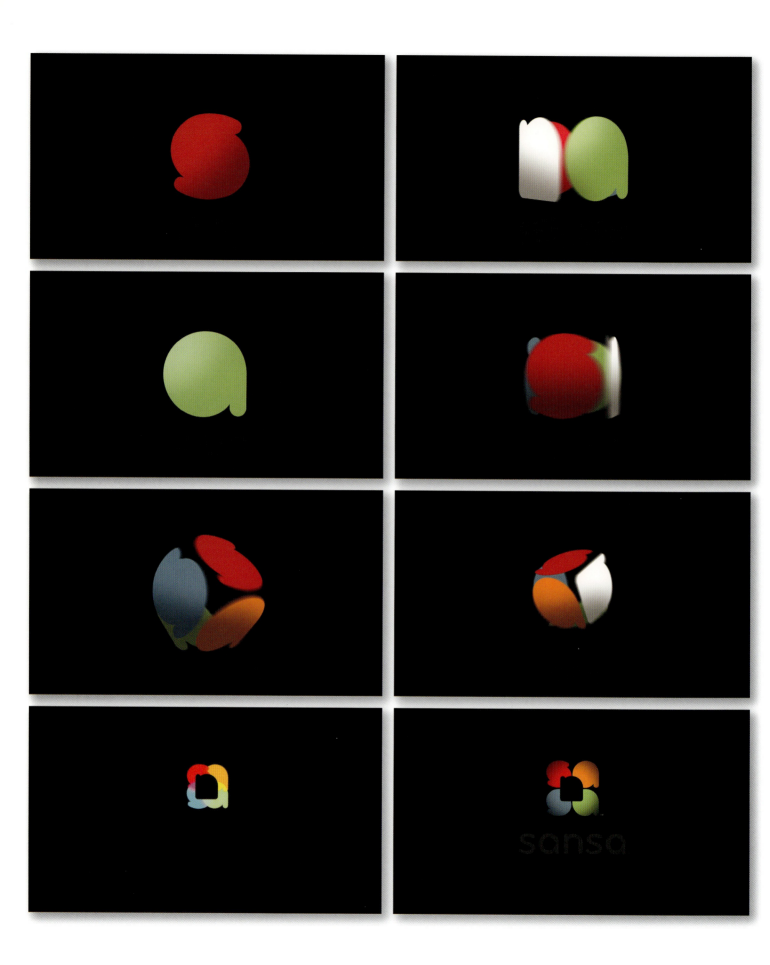

RESIDENTIAL SUPPORT

We provide three types of residential supports: Community Homes, Independent Living, and Community Support. Since our first home opened over 30 years ago, we've placed great importance on the compatability between roommates, support workers, and service providers. Because of our dedicated staff, our 45 clients have been able to reach personal bests that have gone beyond expectations.

Imagine finally being able to go for a drive. To feel the sun on your face as you look out the passenger window. To see the mountains in all their glory.

CALGARY SOCIETY FOR PERSONS WITH DISABILITIES

2008 ANNUAL REPORT

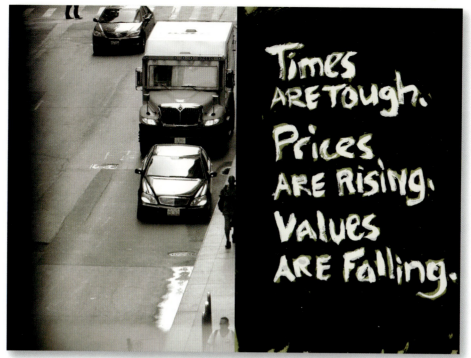

Times ARE TOUGH.
Prices ARE RISING.
Values ARE Falling.

FOR FREE
WITHOUT BUREAUCRACY,
WITHOUT FANFARE,
WITHOUT DEMAND.

OUR VOLUNTEERS ARE THE BEST OF THE LEGAL PROFESSION

CVLS SHINES ON.

It was another busy year at Neenah Paper. Since becoming a separate public company in late 2004, Neenah Paper's strategic vision has centered on profitable growth and transformation. Our plan was to sustain and improve our very profitable, branded fine paper business and to gain scale and enhance technical products. At the same time, we worked on strengthening our pulp operation, making it profitable. We have made significant progress on each of these fronts in 2007, and in the process, continued to reshape our company.

2007 was a year of integration and execution, establishing the groundwork for our future. Following our acquisition of Neenah Germany in late 2006, we implemented a new structure in Technical Products in order to manage this segment as five global business units to take advantage of our new global footprint. We also invested capital in Germany, supporting future growth in filtration, wall covering and other durable printing products. In our fine paper business, the acquisition of the Fox River Paper Company in early March set the stage for a very busy and important year in this segment. We executed a detailed business integration plan, aligning our brands and our distribution network, merging sales and administrative functions, and consolidating our manufacturing footprint. Our remaining pulp operation in Pictou, Nova Scotia achieved record productivity levels and implemented other initiatives to control costs. Finally, we successfully started up Phase II of our ERP (Enterprise Resource Planning) system in the U.S., which drove important change in how we do our jobs and provides us with another tool for improving customer service, operations and supply chain capabilities. As I said, it was a busy year.

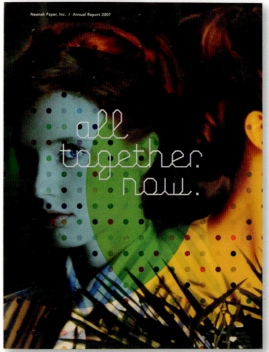

Neenah Paper, Inc. / Annual Report 2007

all together. now.

Profile by Geography 2005
% of total net sales

Rest of World 1%
Asia Pacific 7%
Europe 12%
North America 86%

Profile by Geography 2007
% of total net sales

Rest of World 1%
Asia Pacific 5%
Europe 30%
North America 64%

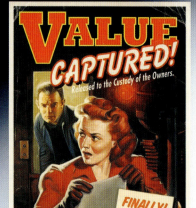

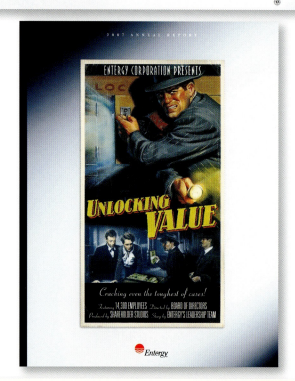

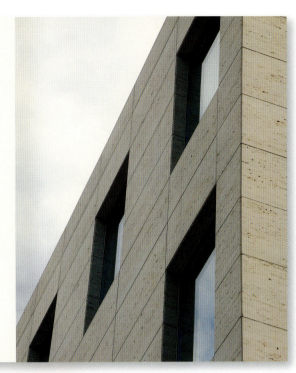

NAPA

BEHIND THE BOTTLE

BILL TUCKER

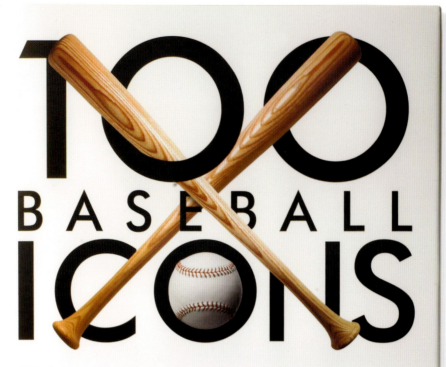

100 BASEBALL ICONS

FROM THE NATIONAL BASEBALL HALL OF FAME AND MUSEUM ARCHIVES

TERRY HEFFERNAN, KIT HINRICHS & DELPHINE HIRASUNA

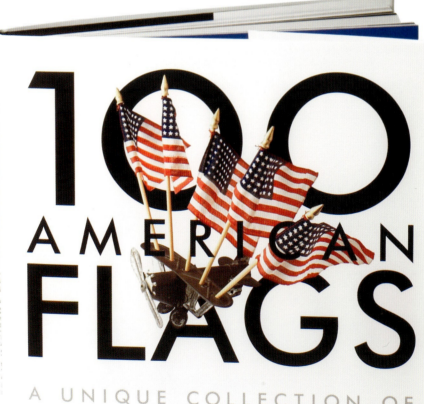

100 AMERICAN FLAGS

A UNIQUE COLLECTION OF OLD GLORY MEMORABILIA

KIT HINRICHS, DELPHINE HIRASUNA & TERRY HEFFERNAN

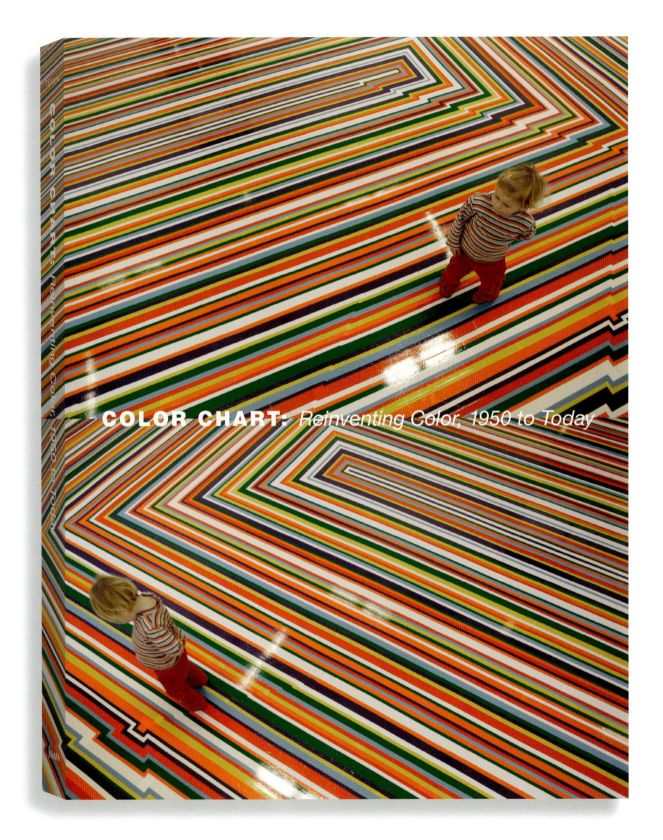

COLOR CHART: *Reinventing Color, 1950 to Today*

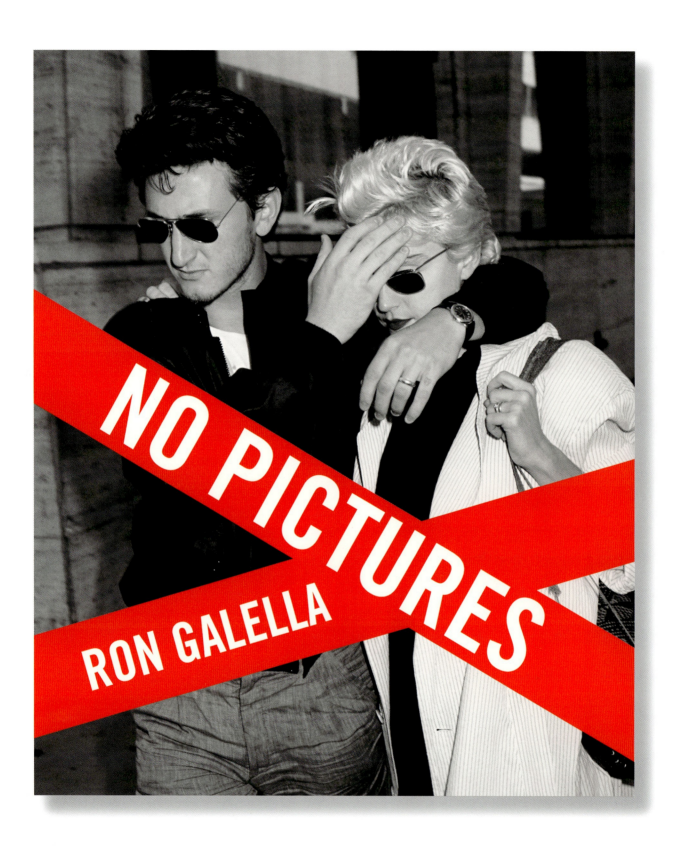

NO PICTURES

RON GALELLA

an R rated look at an X rated industry

naked ambition

michael grecco

Minds at Work.

54% FEMALE

46% MALE

They have an average high school GPA of 3.05.

PROOF

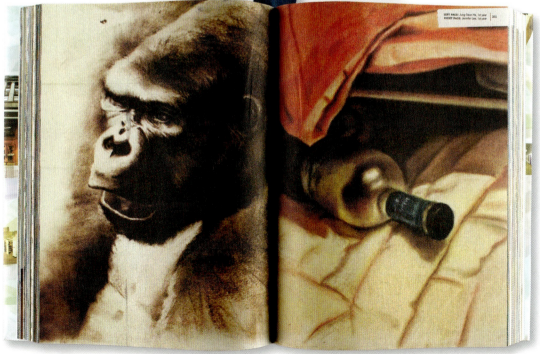

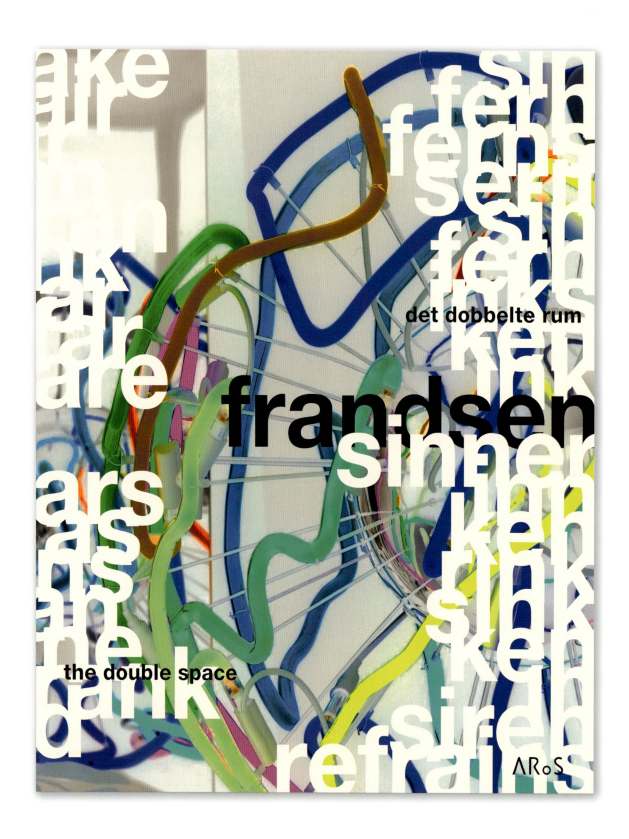

det dobbelte rum

frandsen

the double space

AROS

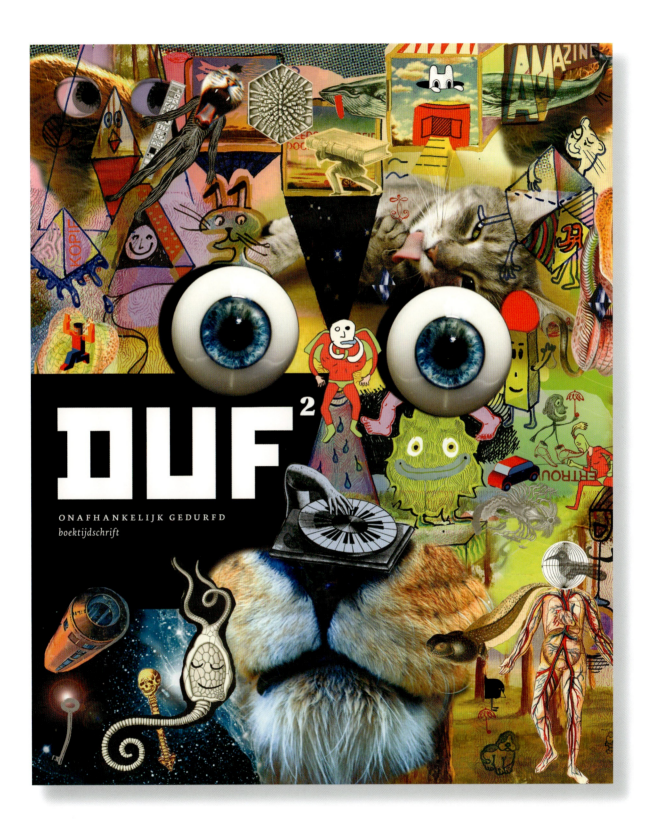

DUF²

ONAFHANKELIJK GEDURFD
boektijdschrift

On Guard

by JUDY BACHRACH
illustrations by TAVIS COBURN

I **T IS ONLY FITTING THAT NICHOLAS BELTRANTE DECIDES TO RECOUNT**
the remarkable details of his event-packed life on June 17, 2008— and not simply because
that date happens to be the former detective's 81st birthday. Back in 1972, June 17 was
also the day of the Watergate break-in at the Democratic National Committee headquarters, an incident that ensnared not only the five burglars who were discovered
attempting to bug the place, but also then-President Richard M. Nixon, who first tried
to cover up the scandal, and subsequently had to resign.

Unsurprisingly to those who know him, ace private eye Nick Beltrante was hired
two days after the burglars were caught in the act. His mission: to debug the Watergate
offices and uncover who among the many volunteers ostensibly helping out Democratic

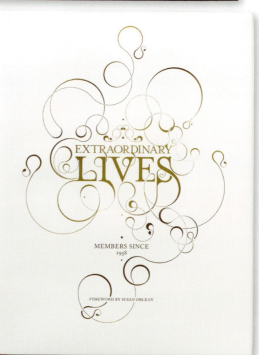

EXTRAORDINARY
LIVES

MEMBERS SINCE
1958

FOREWORD BY SUSAN ORLEAN

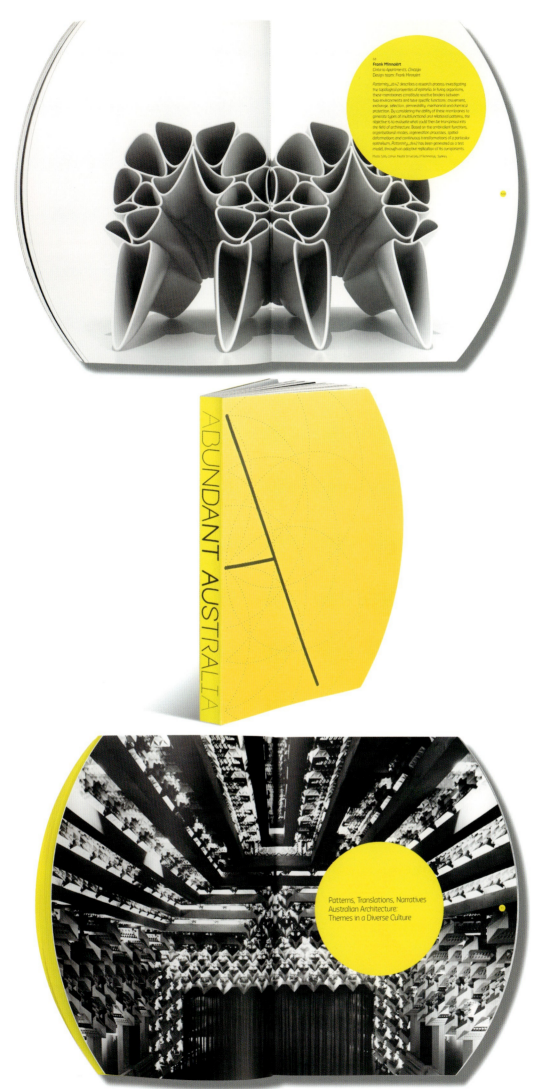

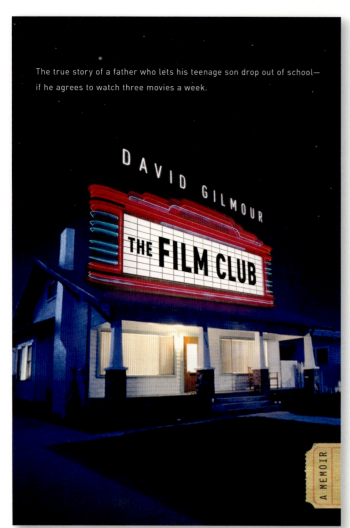

The true story of a father who lets his teenage son drop out of school—
if he agrees to watch three movies a week.

DAVID GILMOUR

THE FILM CLUB

A MEMOIR

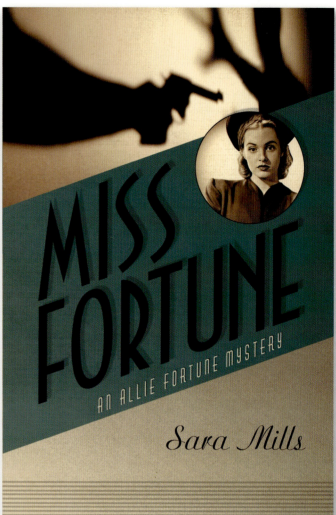

MISS FORTUNE

AN ALLIE FORTUNE MYSTERY

Sara Mills

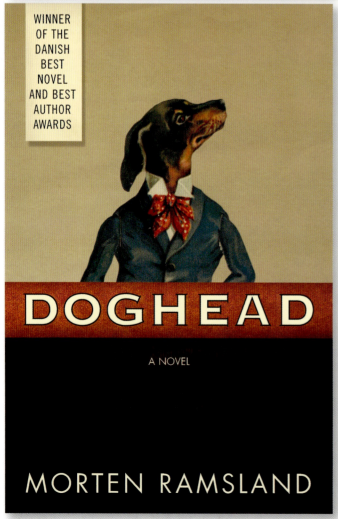

WINNER OF THE DANISH BEST NOVEL AND BEST AUTHOR AWARDS

DOGHEAD

A NOVEL

MORTEN RAMSLAND

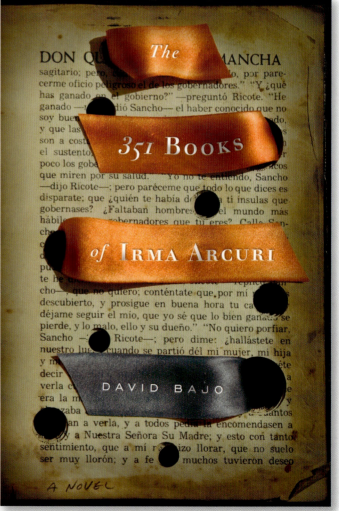

The 351 Books of IRMA ARCURI

DAVID BAJO

A NOVEL

The DesignWorks Group www.thedesignworksgroup.com | Grand Central Publishing
The DesignWorks Group www.thedesignworksgroup.com | Moody Publishers
St. Martin's Press us.macmillan.com/smp.aspx | St. Martin's Press
PENGUIN GROUP (USA) INC. www.us.penguingroup.com | PENGUIN GROUP (USA) INC. | Books46

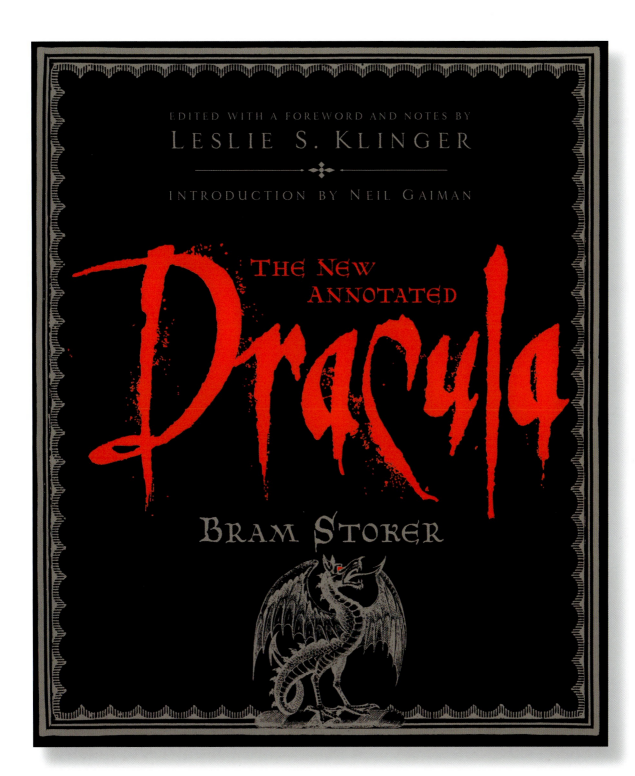

so good....!

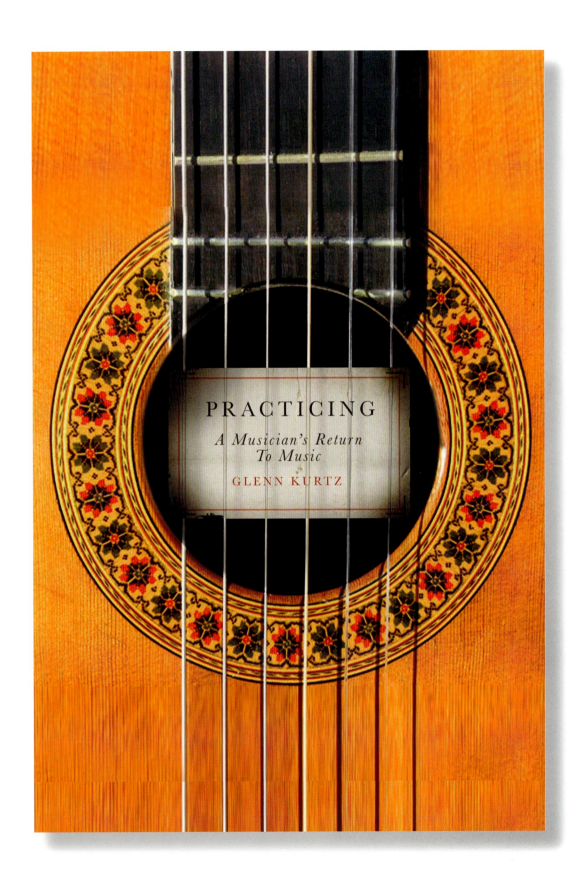

PRACTICING

*A Musician's Return
To Music*

GLENN KURTZ

NetApp®
Go further, faster

Our employees' passion is our greatest asset. We push ourselves and each other to over deliver, setting new standards for service and giving our customers new ways to move their business forward.

Gardening

Paint

DIY

OFFICE CHAIR RELAY

OFFICE GAMES 2008

RECYCLING ROWING

OFFICE GAMES 2008

POST-IT® NOTE FENCING

OFFICE GAMES 2008

FLOPPY DISCUS

OFFICE GAMES 2008

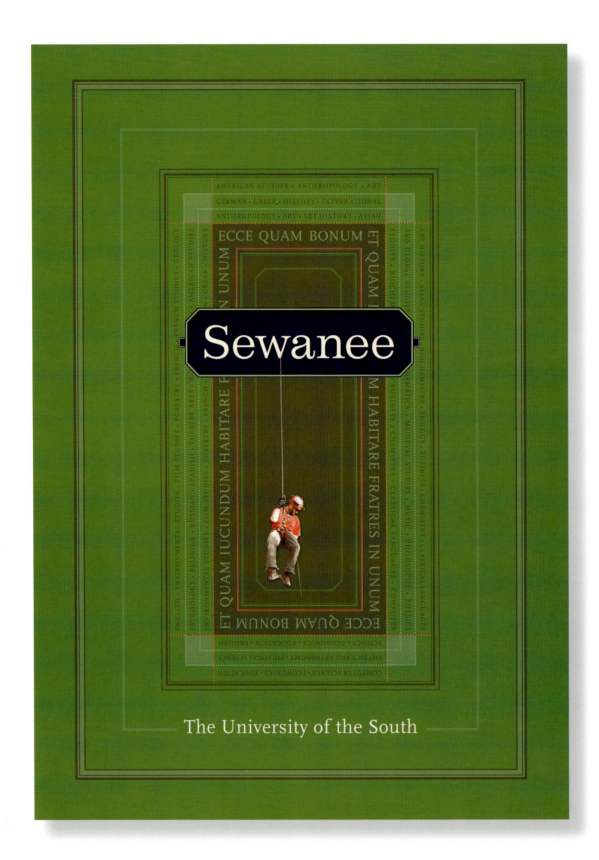

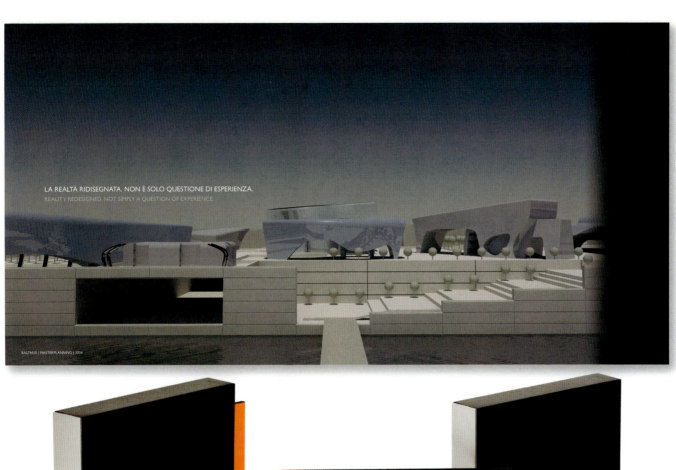

LA REALTÀ RIDISEGNATA. NON È SOLO QUESTIONE DI ESPERIENZA.
REALITY REDESIGNED. NOT SIMPLY A QUESTION OF EXPERIENCE.

BALTHUS | MASTERPLANNING | 2004

DESIGN
LIKE
MAGIC

CENTROPOLIS DESIGN

EXPERTS IN DESIGN, ARCHITECTURE, INTERIORS AND DETAILS

FABULA SOUTH BEACH | INTERIORS DESIGN | 2007-2009

Day in and day out, it's all Lynx Opaque never fails. and from mill to mill, Opaque for trouble-free smooth, steady and of exhaust pipes on the

about consistency. And From month to month, there's no beating Lynx performance that's as satisfying as the sound open road.

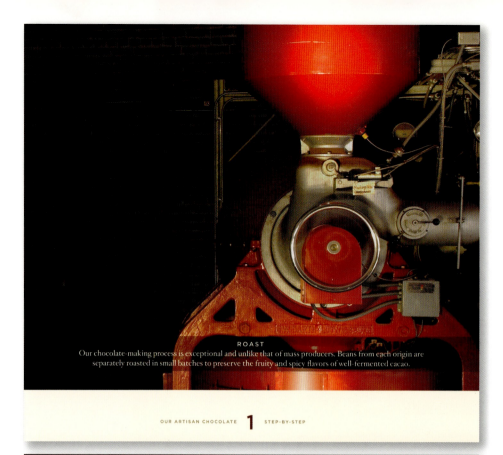

ROAST

Our chocolate-making process is exceptional and unlike that of mass producers. Beans from each origin are separately roasted in small batches to preserve the fruity and spicy flavors of well-fermented cacao.

OUR ARTISAN CHOCOLATE **1** STEP-BY-STEP

SCHARFFEN BERGER®

CHOCOLATE MAKER

REFINE

We grind our beans into chocolate liquor using a vintage European mélangeur (granite mill). Then we refine the liquor with purified sugar and whole vanilla beans in a machine called a conche-refiner for up to 60 hours to ensure a smooth and delicious chocolate.

OUR ARTISAN CHOCOLATE **3** STEP-BY-STEP

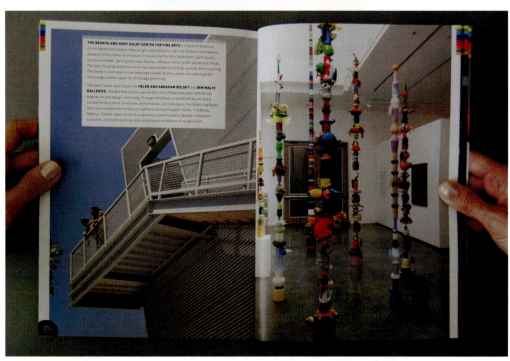

SPACES FROM
THE HANNON RICHARDS COLLECTION

VOLUME ONE

ELEVATE
DESIRE

HANNON RICHARDS
ARCHITECTURAL COLLECTIONS

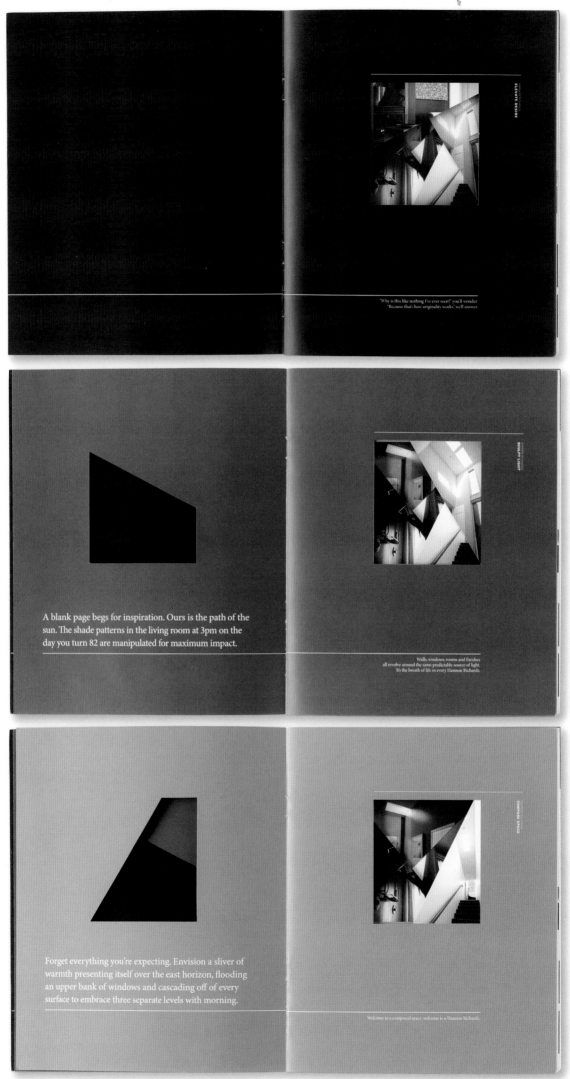

A blank page begs for inspiration. Ours is the path of the sun. The shade patterns in the living room at 3pm on the day you turn 82 are manipulated for maximum impact.

Walls, windows, rooms and finishes
all revolve around the same predictable source of light.
It's the breath of life in every Hannon Richards.

Forget everything you're expecting. Envision a sliver of warmth presenting itself over the east horizon, flooding an upper bank of windows and cascading off of every surface to embrace three separate levels with morning.

Welcome to a composed space, welcome to a Hannon Richards.

Start Out on the Right Foot

Push the Right Buttons

Get a Clear View of Your Product

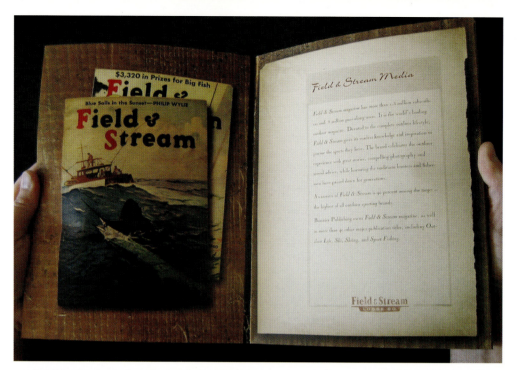

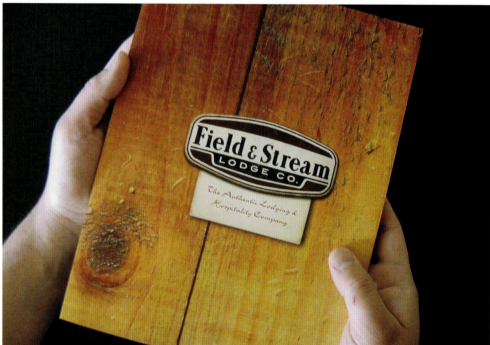

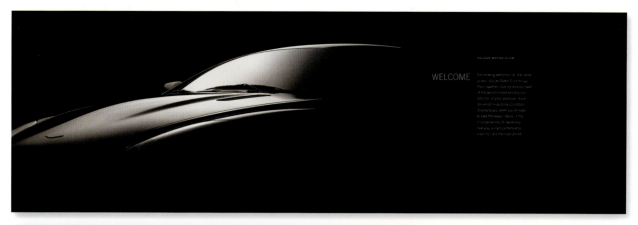

WELCOME

ACCESS

ADVANTAGE

EXCLUSIVITY

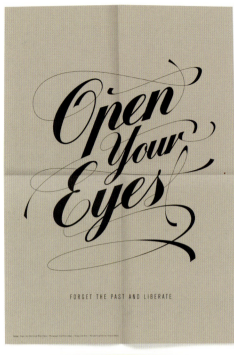

Open Your Eyes

FORGET THE PAST AND LIBERATE

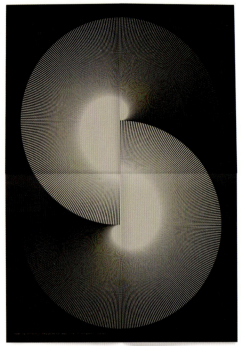

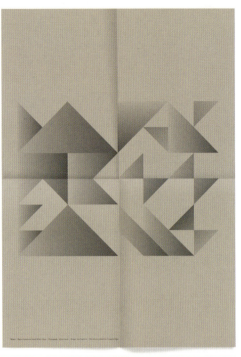

February

March

July

August

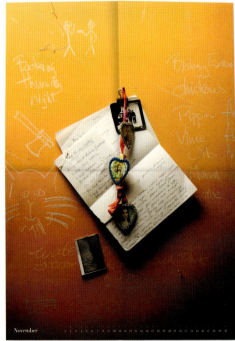

November

December

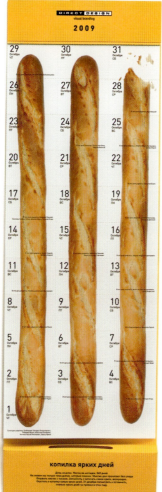

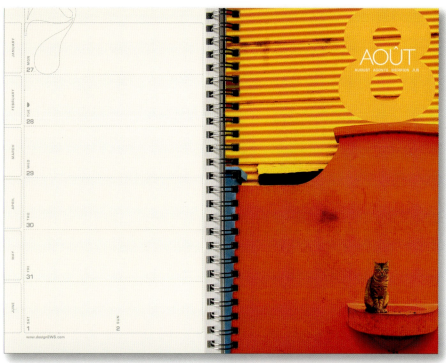

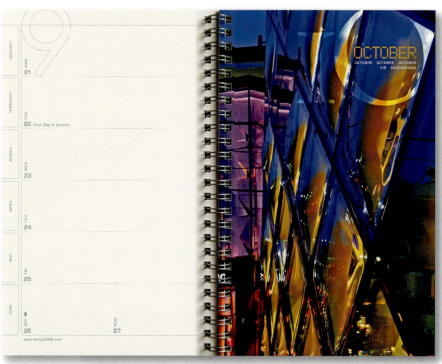

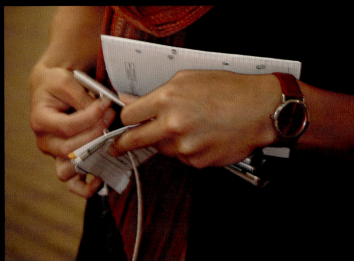

HARLEY-DAVIDSON®
2009 CUSTOM VEHICLE OPERATIONS™ MOTORCYCLES

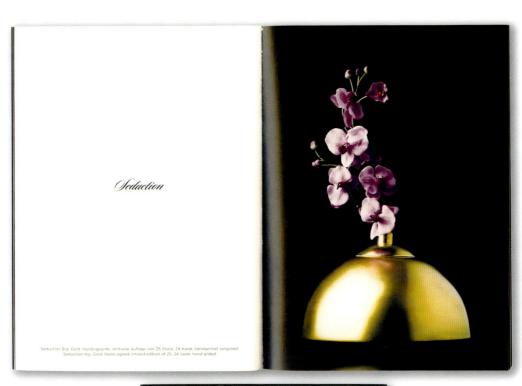

Seduction

Seduction Big. Gold. Handsignierte, limiterte Auflage von 25 Stück, 24 Karat, handgemalt vergoldet
Seduction big. Gold. Hand signed, limited edition of 25, 24 carat, hand gilded

Seduction Small. Platin. Handsignierte, limiterte Auflage von 250 Stück, 99% reinstes Platin, handgemalt
Seduction Small. Platinum. Hand signed, limited edition of 250, 99% pure Platinum, hand gilded

LIDA BADAY

IL BIANCO

LINO

E
IL NERO

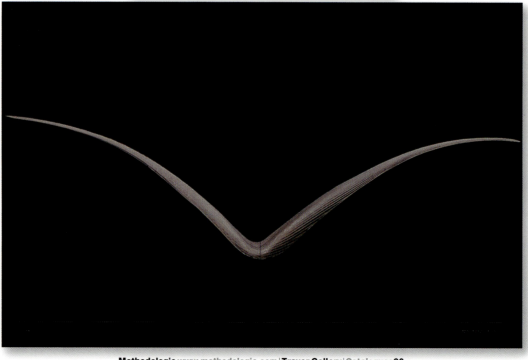

HARMONY IN CONTRAST

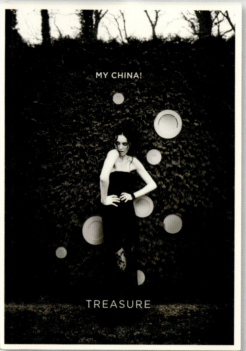

MY CHINA!

TREASURE

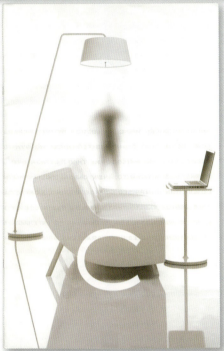

new editions by hans kaufeld

typ 1

typ 8

EX CESS 80s

PHOTOGRAPHY *NAGI SAKAI*
STYLING *MASAYO KISHI*

110

BOTH IMAGES Dress, Manish Arora

111

Camouflage

Nº1 — THE SHOES ISSUE
FALL—WINTER 2008/2009
MUST—HAVE SHOES—ALICE DELLAL
EXCESS 80s—BELA BORSODI

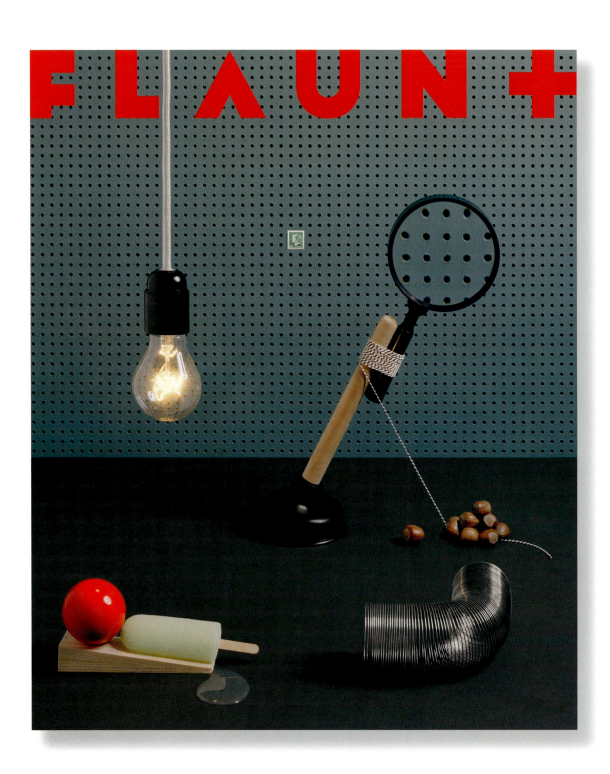

the sweet

T
S

S
science

O
S
of swimsuits

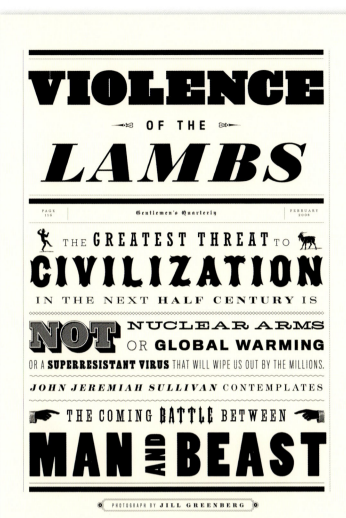

VIOLENCE OF THE LAMBS

PAGE 116 | Gentlemen's Quarterly | FEBRUARY 2008

THE **GREATEST THREAT** TO **CIVILIZATION** IN THE NEXT HALF CENTURY IS **NOT** NUCLEAR ARMS OR **GLOBAL WARMING** OR A **SUPERRESISTANT VIRUS** THAT WILL WIPE US OUT BY THE MILLIONS.

JOHN JEREMIAH SULLIVAN CONTEMPLATES

THE COMING **BATTLE** BETWEEN

MAN AND BEAST

PHOTOGRAPH BY **JILL GREENBERG**

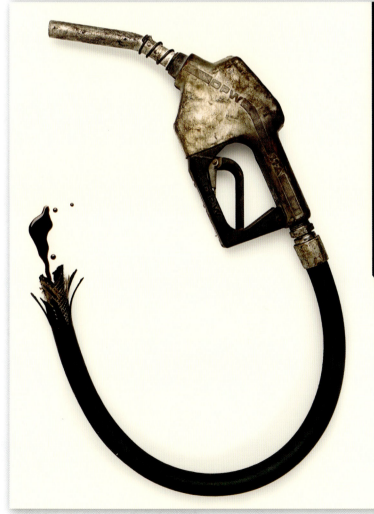

PHOTOGRAPHS BY
Christopher Griffith

GQ.COM 151 8/08

→ Think $4 for a gallon of gas is screwing with your summer? Wait until you hear about something called *peak oil*. According to a growing number of experts—and we're not just talking about conspiracy wackos here—we're on the brink of an economic crisis that could lead to, well, the end of life as we know it. **Benjamin Kunkel** investigates just how scary things are about to become

World Without Oil, Amen

Digital (n.) a showing information in the form of an electronic display

Editor
Lakshmi Bhaskaran
lakshmi@dandad.co.uk

Sub Editor
Hester Lacey

Design & Art Director
Vince Frost
Anthony Donovan
Frost Design, Sydney
www.frostdesign.com.au

3D Design
Gary Nicholson

Advertising
Katherine Howells
katherine@dandad.co.uk

W: D&AD
9 Graphite Square,
Vauxhall Walk
London SE11 5EE
T: +44 (0) 20 7840 1111
E: ampersand@dandad.co.uk
W: www.dandad.co.uk

Printed by Beacon Press
using puregreen®
environmental print
technology

'&' is printed on
100% Recycled Paper

© D&AD 2008

Cover Image
Paul Belford

Contributors
James Biber, Hannah Booth
Patrick Burgoyne
Chris Clarke, Liz Hancock

Welcome to Ampersand Volume 3: On Digital. Digital design remains one of the fastest-growing and evolving fields within the creative industries. Over the next three issues we'll be focusing on the latest developments and talking to many of the rising stars of the digital world. Speaking of rising stars, in this issue D&AD's incoming president Simon Waterfall is Q&A'd (p04), on page 15 Hannah Booth profiles four digital design studios currently making their mark, and, in the wake of a world-wide severely misguided attempt to save the planet by stamping a mammoth carbon footprint across the globe, Liz Hancock joins us once again with a timely (and helpful) eco-update (p34). I am also delighted to welcome on board Chris Clarke from Digitas as our latest columnist (p25) and to welcome back Patrick Burgoyne for a third term (p05). Elsewhere, Pentagram partner James Biber takes us on a multi-tasking whistle-stop tour of New York (p36) and we challenge key industry figures to fly the flag in the Gallery (p26). Enjoy ...

Lakshmi Bhaskaran, editor
If you've any thoughts or comments about this issue, drop me a line at lakshmi@dandad.co.uk

---

This year the Alzheimer's Society sponsored a brief entitled The Fight Against Dementia, inviting students to use the power of photography to communicate the many facets of the disease. Vanessa Norwood and Pat Butler from East Lancashire Institute of Higher Education took first place with the following series of thought-provoking images, described by Al Young, D&AD's Education chairman, as simply 'haunting' ...

A-ward (n.) a prize given in recognition of merit or achievement

Editor
Lakshmi Bhaskaran
lakshmi@dandad.co.uk

Managing Editor
Tiffany Foster
tiffany@dandad.co.uk

Sub Editor
Hester Lacey

Design & Art Direction
Vince Frost,
Anthony Donovan &
Adrian Hing
Frost Design, Sydney/London
www.frostdesign.com.au

3D Design
Kevin Lee

Advertising
Katherine Howells
katherine@dandad.co.uk

W: D&AD
9 Graphite Square
Vauxhall Walk
London SE11 5EE
T: +44 (0) 20 7840 1111
E: ampersand@dandad.co.uk
W: www.dandad.co.uk

Printed by Beacon Press
using puregreen®
environmental print
technology

'&' is printed on
100% Recycled Paper

© D&AD 2008

Cover Image
'Moody' Sir Bernardo's by
Battle Bogle Hegarty
Photographer Kiran Master
Nominated for a D&AD
Yellow Pencil in
Writing for Advertising

Contributors
Hannah Booth
Patrick Burgoyne
Pat Butler
Chris Clarke
Nick Howe
Vanessa Norwood
Greg Quinton
Tamsin Valentino
Al Young

It's that time of year again: we look back at another 12 months of outstanding creativity and see who walked away with this year's stash of Pencils. With a Black Pencil under his belt, Greg Quinton shares the highlights (and lowlights) of his 2008 Awards experience (p.06), while Al Young offers his thoughts on this year's Student Awards (p.23). As D&AD's Student Awards celebrates its 30th year, Hannah Booth catches up with some past winners to find out how their careers have progressed (p.30). This issue we look to Liverpool, the 2008 European Capital of Culture, for our Creative City Guide, with Tamsin Valentino and Nick Howe (p.37). Elsewhere, Chris Clarke looks towards a post-superstar world (p.22) and Q&A introduces your new D&AD president, Garrick Hamm (p.04). Enjoy.

Lakshmi Bhaskaran, editor
If you've any thoughts or comments about this issue, drop me a line at lakshmi@dandad.co.uk

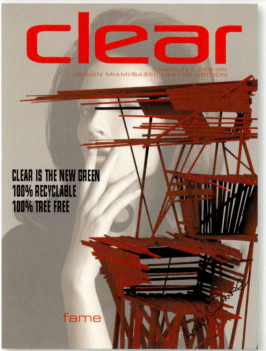

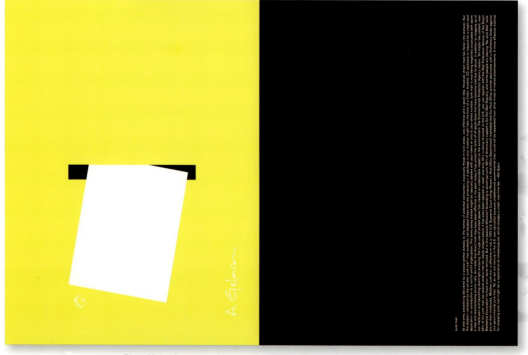

PREFIX PHOTO

A Publication of Prefix Institute of Contemporary Art

Prefix
Photo
18:
Technology
and the Body

Volume 9, Number 2
Display Until April 30
$18 CA $14.95 US
£8.95 €12.95

DEAR
DAVE,

REED + RADER

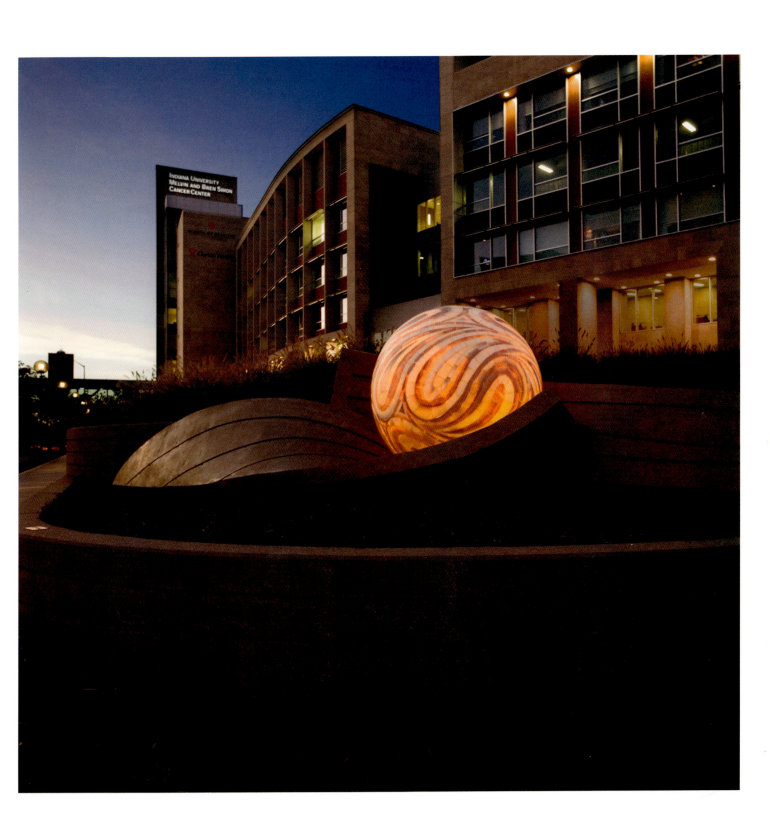

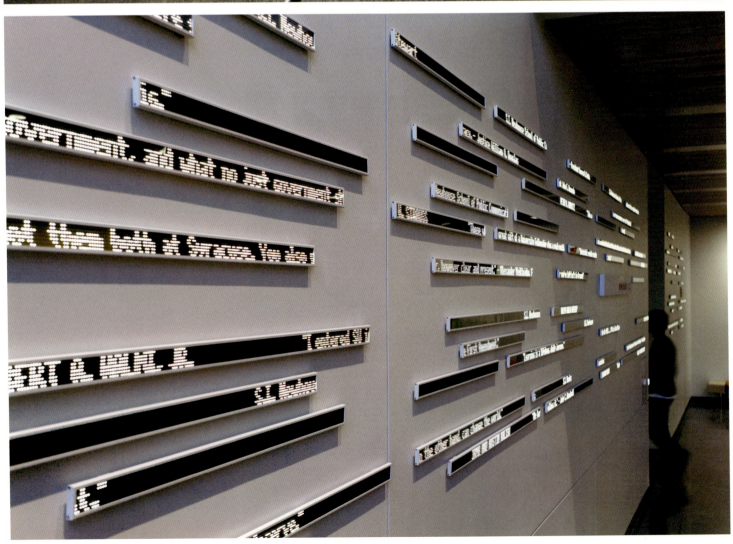

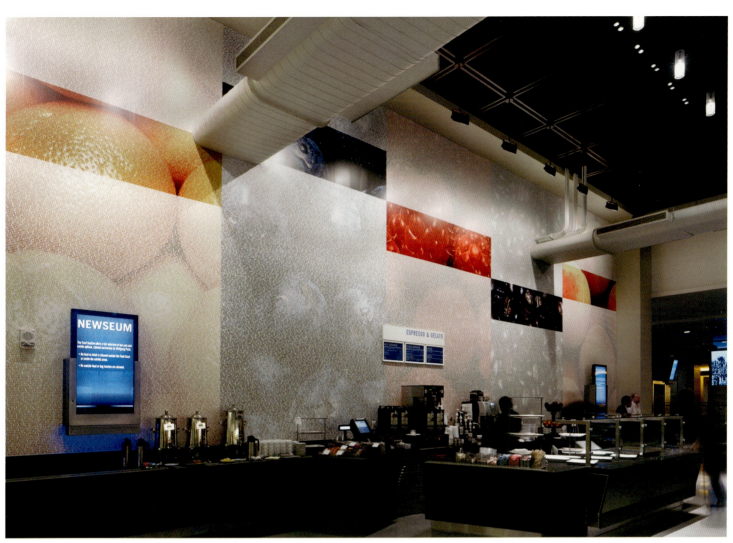

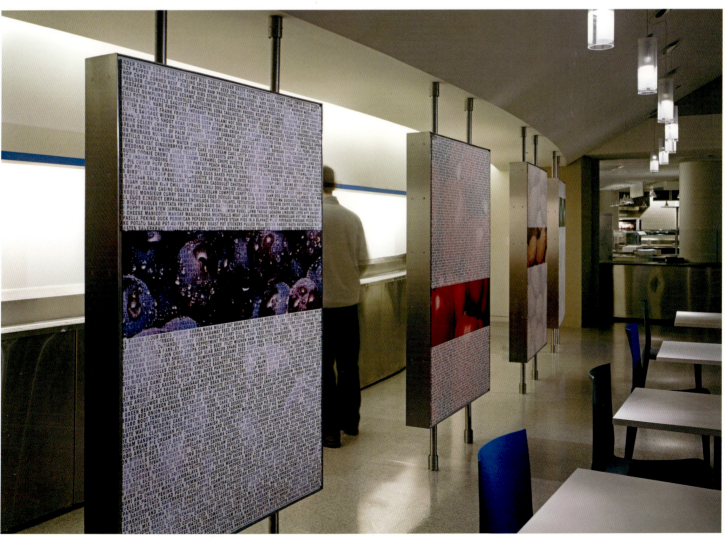

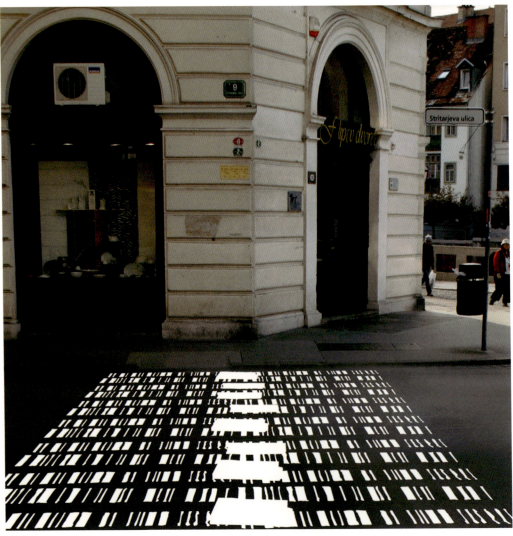

ROBOTS

Domo arigato, Mr. Roboto

Thank you very much, Mr. Roboto

For doing the jobs that nobody wants to

And thank you very much, Mr. Roboto

For helping me escape just when I needed to...

–Dennis DeYoung, Styx

LONG MAY SHE WAVE
A Graphic History of the American Flag

"Consider the postage stamp, its usefulness consists in

A
IS FOR
ADVERTISING COVERS

B
IS FOR
BISECT

C
IS FOR
CINDERELLA STAMP

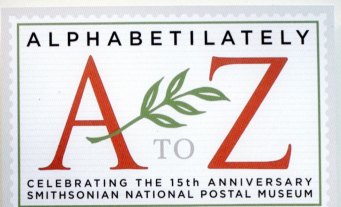

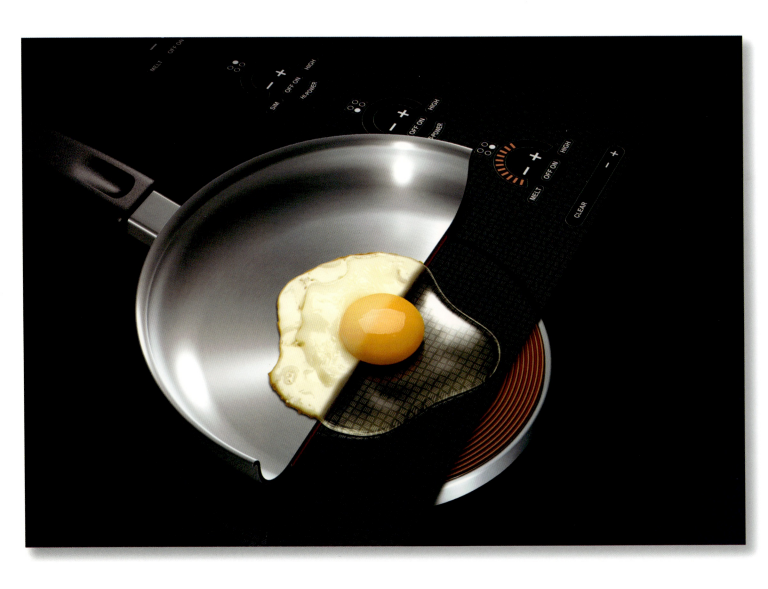

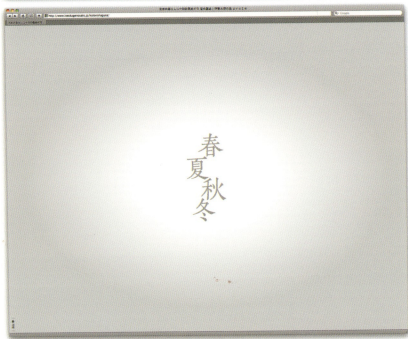

think/thing

Transferring data from www.thinkmoreinc.com...

think/thing

products
research
software
architecture
publications
who we are
awards
press
things we like
open source design

contact

nestt
OUiP! baby
OUiP! kids
OUiP! rehab
OUiP! paint
slenda lamp
baby lounge
hanukah menorah
loudspeaker 1
loudspeaker 2
cd transport
phonograph 1
phonograph 2
q clock
pen

Transferring data from www.thinkmoreinc.com...

think/thing

Transferring data from www.thinkmoreinc.com...

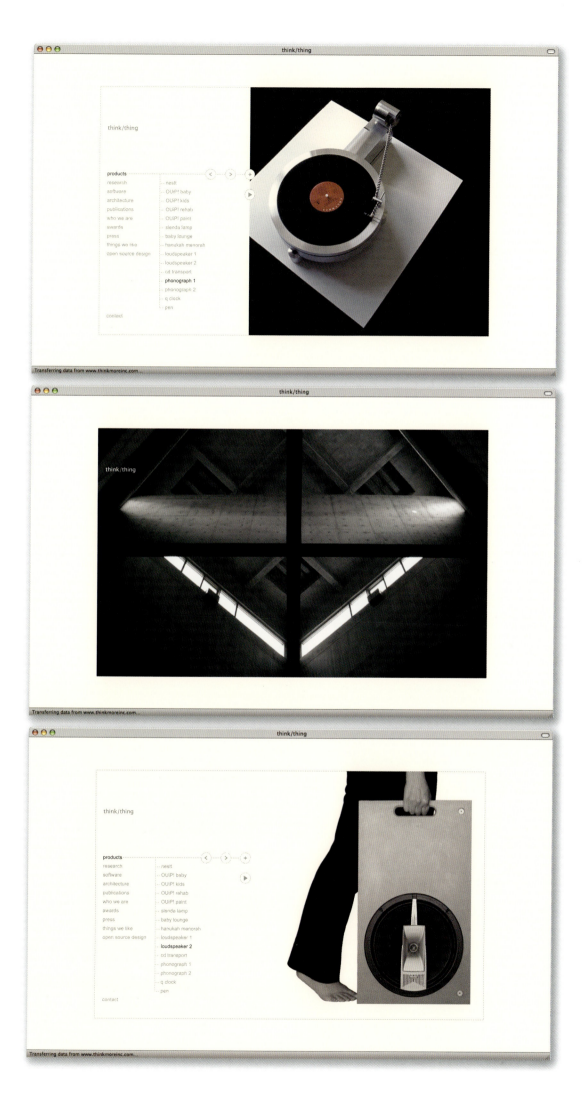

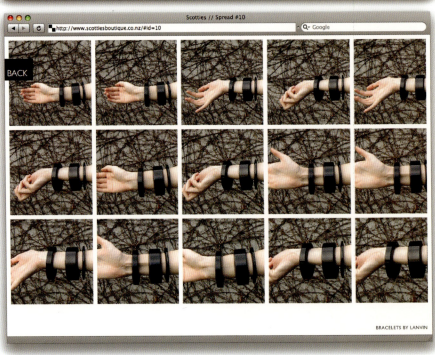

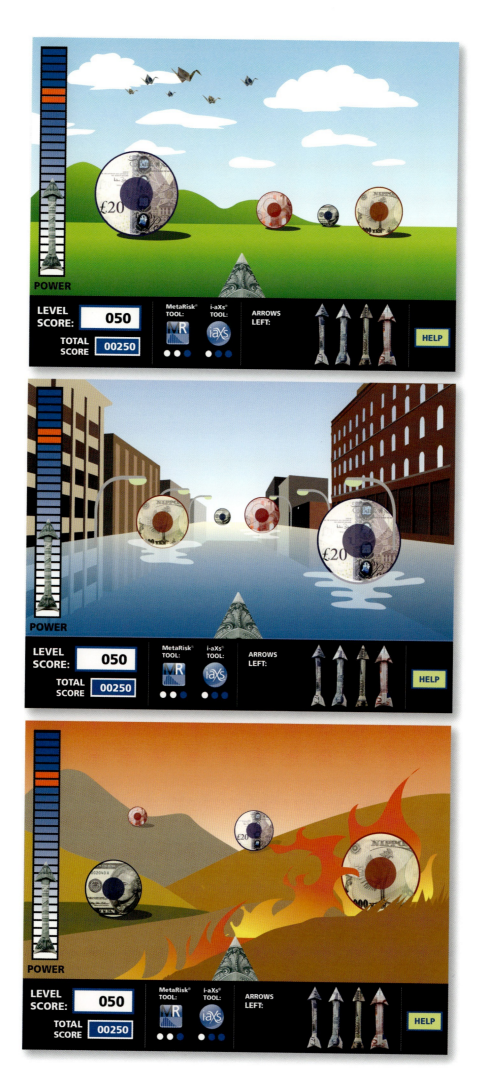

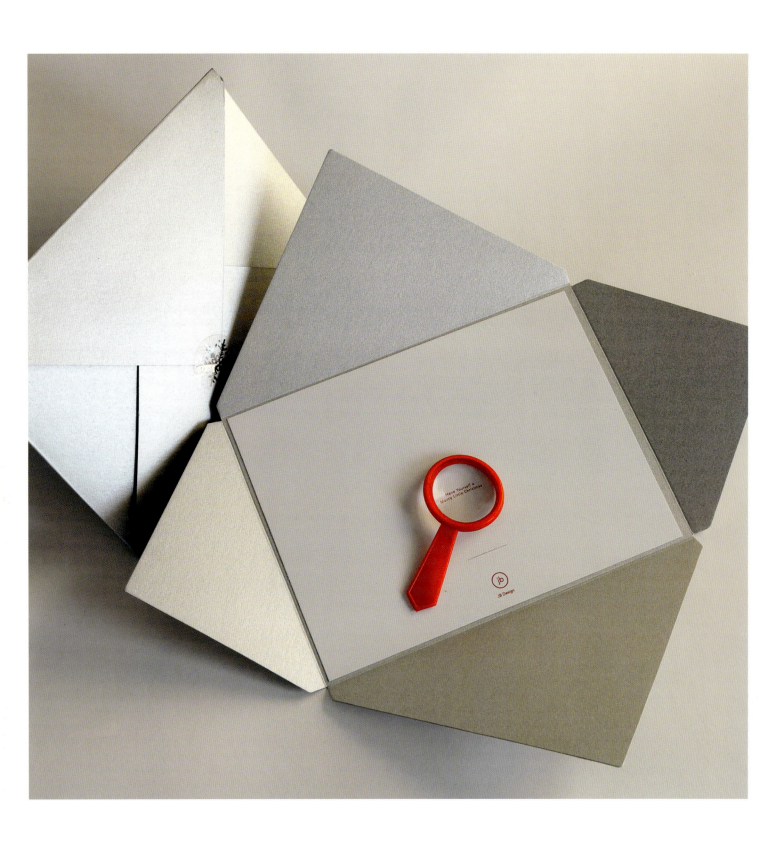

"Here's Johnny!" 2

John Buckland requests the pleasure of your company.

"Go ahead make my day!" 3

For an evening of feasting and frolics to celebrate his 50th birthday.

"Here's looking at you, kid." 4

All guests should dress up as their favourite on screen celebrity.

"The only way to get through it is if we all work together as a team. And that means you do what I say!" 5

Please register your chosen identity @ baftaparty.com.

"There can be only one." 6

Act quickly to avoid disappointment, as your chosen character may already be taken.

"It's showtime!" 7

The party will start at 6.45pm, Dinner 7.30pm prompt, Carriages 12.30am in The David Lean Room, BAFTA, 195 Piccadilly, London, W1

"You have twenty seconds to comply." 8

RSVP: mail@johnbuckland.com no later than the 15th June 2008

"It's gonna be groovy baby!" 9

Johnny eagerly awaits confirmation of your attendance @ baftaparty.com

celebrating extraordinary young leaders

JOHN P. & ANNE WELSH McNULTY FOUNDATION
1300 THIRD STREET SOUTH, SUITE 300, NAPLES, FLORIDA 34102

JOHN P. McNULTY PRIZE

coal.

goh yong yau

coal creative consultants pte ltd
14b smith street singapore 058928

t: +65 6557 0446
d: +65 6557 0857
f: +65 6557 0639
e: yongyau.goh@coal.com.sg

coal creative consultants pte ltd • 14b smith street singapore 058928 • tel: +65 6557 0446 • fax: +65 6557 0639 • www.coal.com.sg

coal creative consultants pte ltd • 14b smith street singapore 058928 • tel: +65 6557 0446 • fax: +65 6557 0639 • www.coal.com.sg

coal.

Webster Design Associates www.websterdesign.com | **Airlite Plastics Co.**
Karen Lukas-Hardy Design GA, United States | **Verbal-Visual Framework**
Michael Schwab Studio www.michaelschwab.com | **Denver Mountain Parks**
AG Creative www.agcreative.ca | **Drake Wellington**
Sibley/Peteet Design www.spdaustin.com | **Tôrchon Catering** | Logos **161**

SLCE

presh

Hornall Anderson www.hornallanderson.com | **Holland America (Canaletto Logo)**
TAXI CANADA INC www.taxi.ca | **Brownstone Book Company**
Colle + McVoy www.collemcvoy.com | **Field and Stream**
Hornall Anderson www.hornallanderson.com | **Holland America (Slice Logo)**
UNIT design collective www.unitcollective.com | **Presh Jewelry** | **Logos165**

CLEVELANDS WAGYU

PEDIGREES *from* PROVEN GENETICS

Hornall Anderson www.hornallanderson.com | **Coffee Bean & Tea Leaf**
MacLaren McCann Calgary www.maclaren.com | **Harrison Pipelines**
Melissa Collins | Graphic Design Bendemeer, NSW Australia | **Clevelands Wagyu**
Bailey Lauerman www.baileylauerman.com | **Mission Bean Coffee**
Sibley/Peteet Design www.spdaustin.com | **Barton Spring Edwards Aquifer Conservation District** | Logos**166**

P H

THE REAGAN LIBRARY
SIMI VALLEY · CALIFORNIA

okooko™

Jessica Campbell www.more-than-skin-deep.com | **Tru-Way Metal Fabrication**
Saatchi Design Worldwide www.saatchi.com | **Penny Hay Limited**
Siegel+Gale www.siegelgale.com | **Ronald Reagan Library**
Saatchi Design Worldwide www.saatchi.com | **Design Mobel**
Strømme Throndsen Design www.stdesign.no | **Natural** | Logos **168**

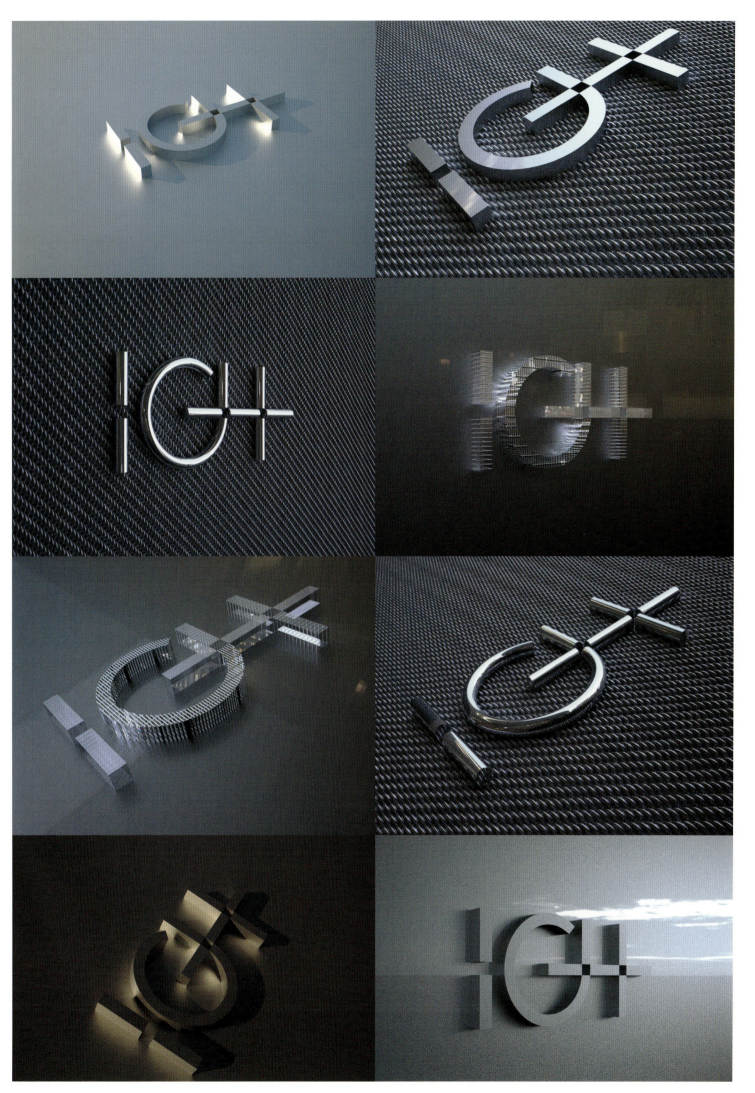

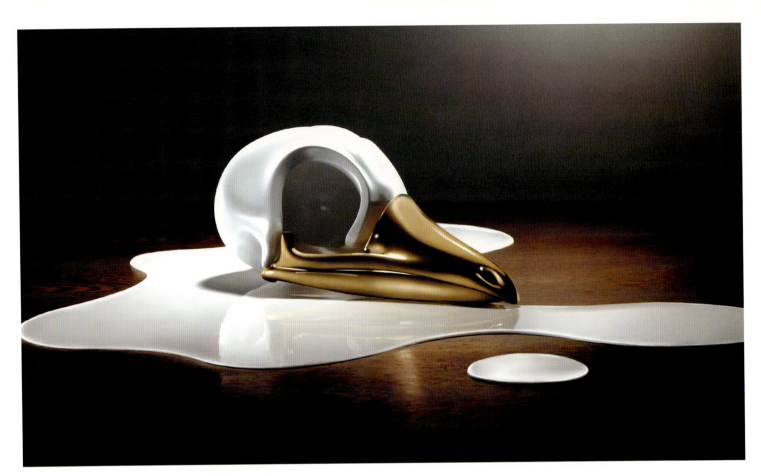

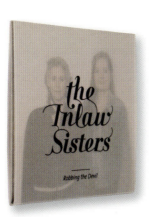

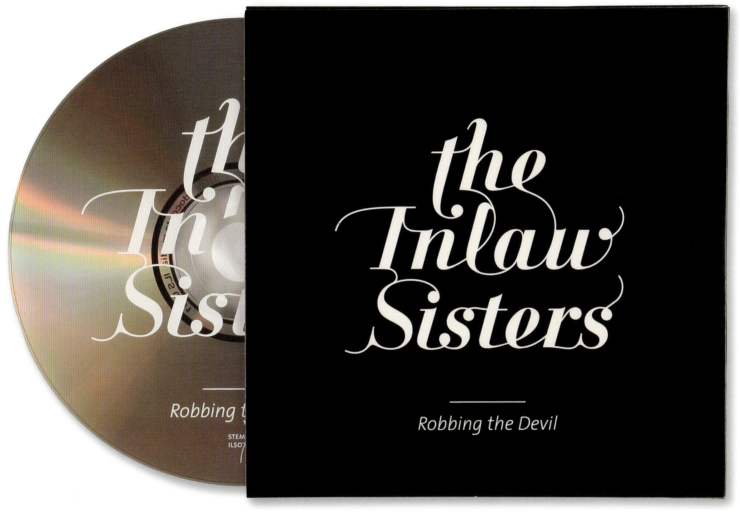

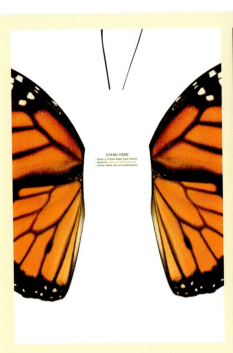

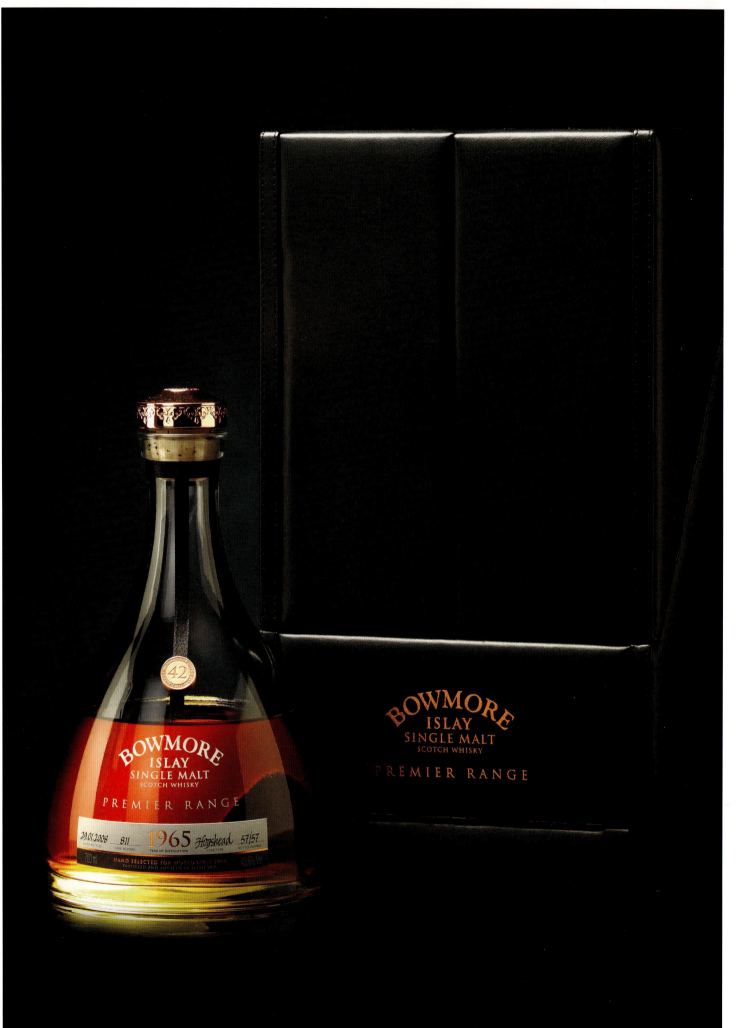

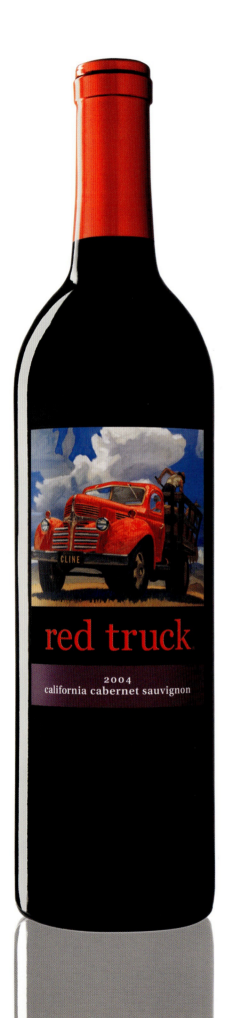

CALI 351

NAPA VALLEY CABERNET SAUVIGNON

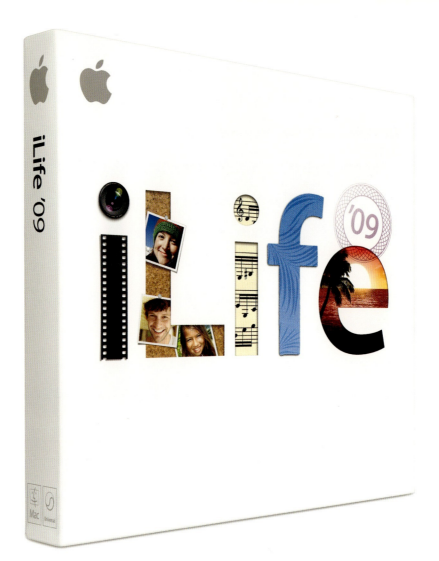

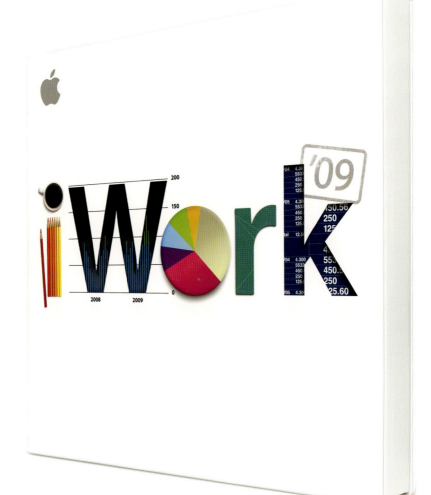

MacBook Pro

15-inch LED-backlit widescreen notebook

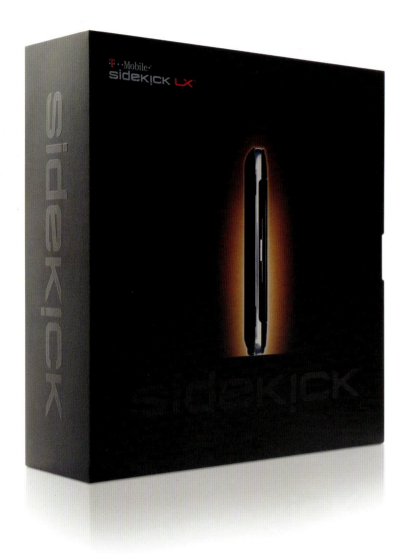
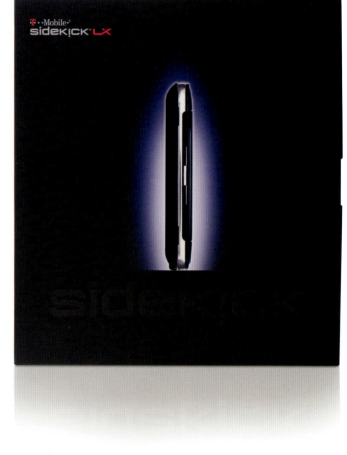

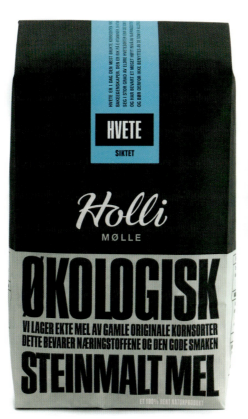

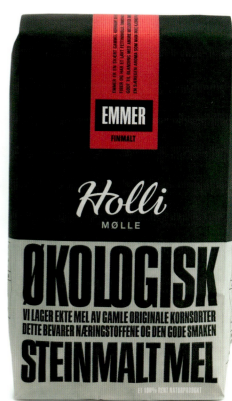

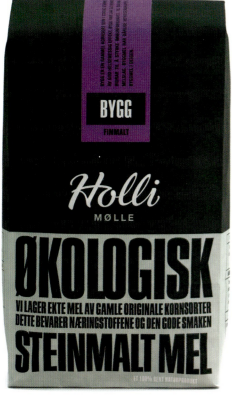

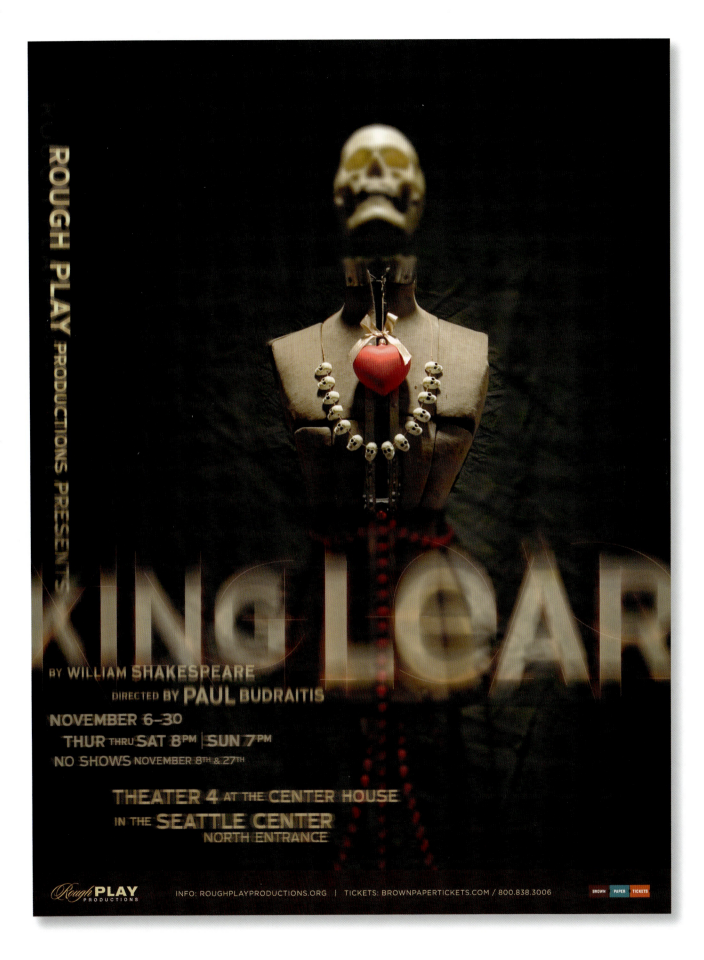

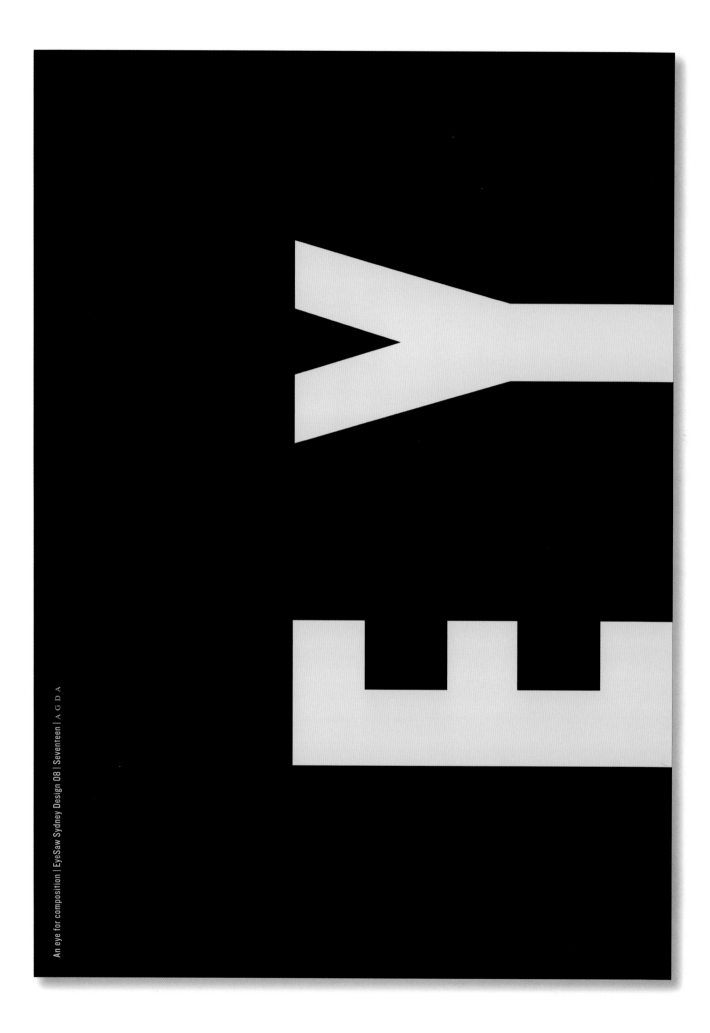

An eye for composition | EyeSaw Sydney Design 08 | Seventeen | A G D A

iPod nano

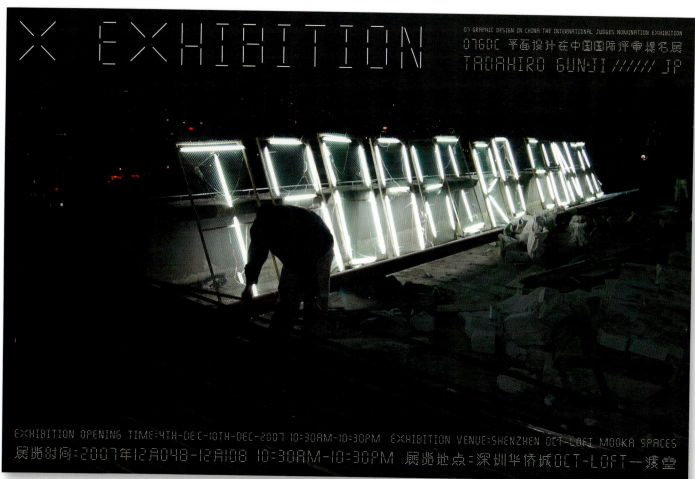

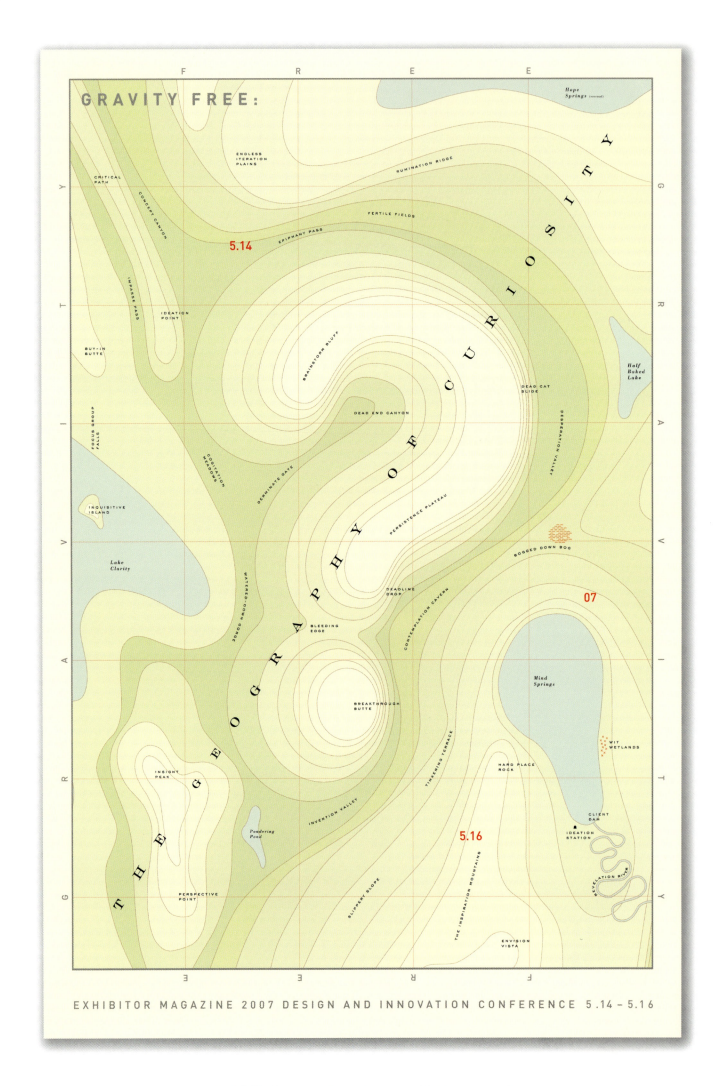

THE NORTHWEST ARKANSAS
ART DIRECTORS CLUB
PROUDLY PRESENTS
PENTAGRAM PARTNER
DJ STOUT
NOVEMBER 7TH, 2008
DICKSON STREET THEATER
FAYETTEVILLE, ARKANSAS
DOORS OPEN 6:30 PM
SHOW STARTS 7:30 PM
STUDENTS FREE
MEMBERS $5
NON-MEMBERS $15

PHOTOGRAPH BY RANDAL FORD

UNBOUND
AT MAMMOTH

MICAH SHAPIRO
FRONTSIDE 720
MAMMOTH UNBOUND
TERRAIN PARK

04.21.08

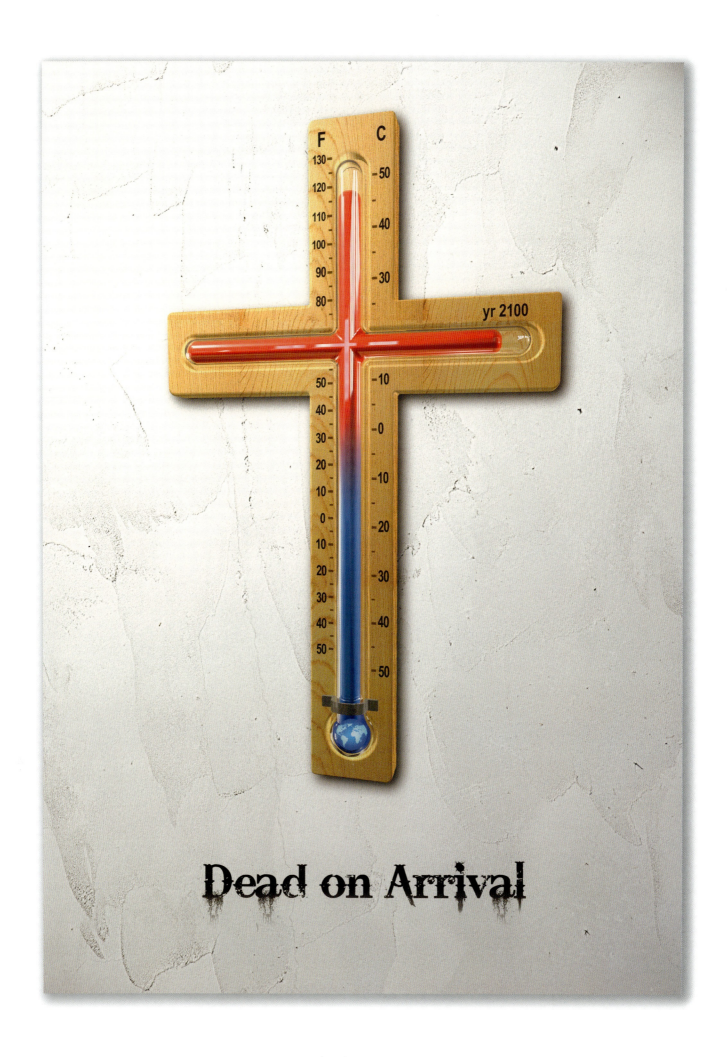

Nutrition Facts

Obesity will soon replace
smoking
as Canada's number one
health problem

Think
before you eat

Dietitians of Canada
www.dietitians.ca

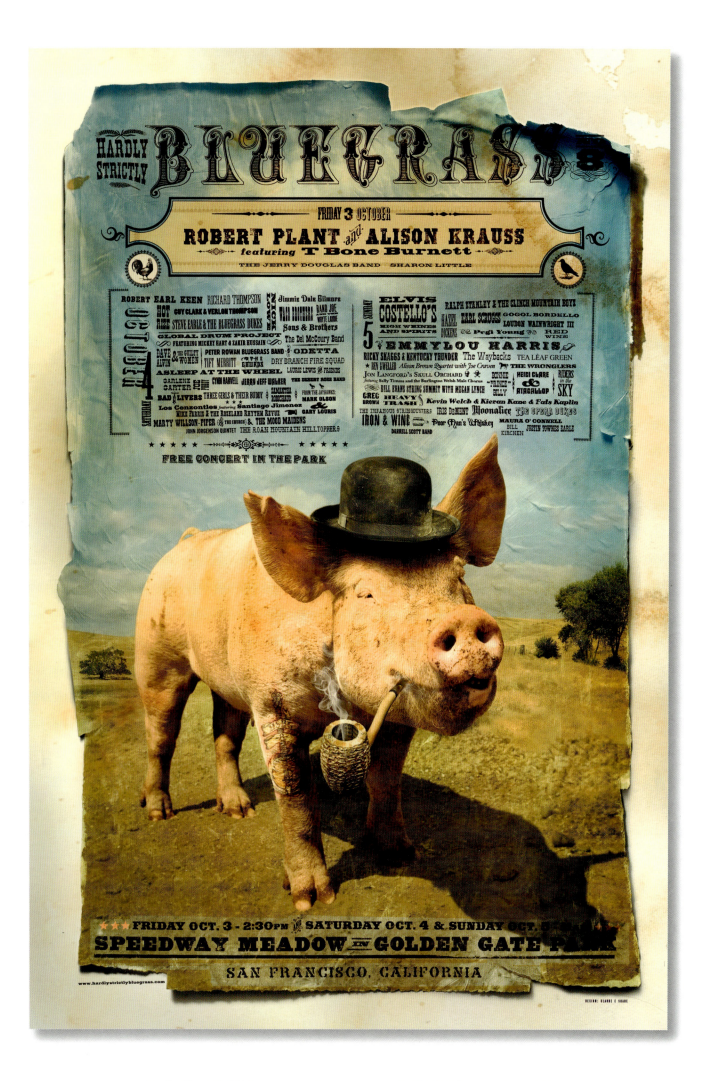

JAMES HACKETT BROADCASTING SOON

FRIDAY 03 04 08 1PM | LEVEL 11 15 BLUE ST

YUN
I
SANG

1917

1995

ㅇᄫ ㄴ
ㅇ ㅣ
ㅅ ㅏ ㅇ

90

2007

ART

SERVING
CAPITALISM

Goodby Silverstein & Partners

Sitting Pretty

The PKO Chair
Designer **Poul Kjærholm**
Country **Denmark**
Manufactured **Fritz Hansen**

Poul Kjærholm designed the
PKO Chair in Denmark in 1952.
Constructed from two lacquered
timber shells the design was so
complex that it was not put into
production until 1997, when 600
individually numbered pieces were
manufactured.

Poster **Hoyne Design**
Photography **Dean Tirkot**

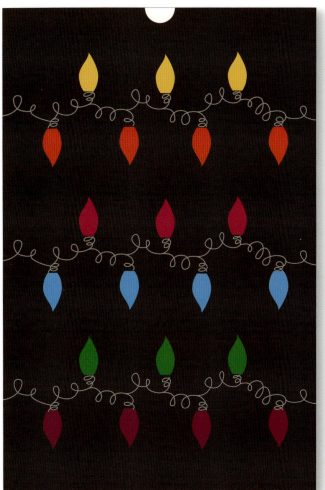

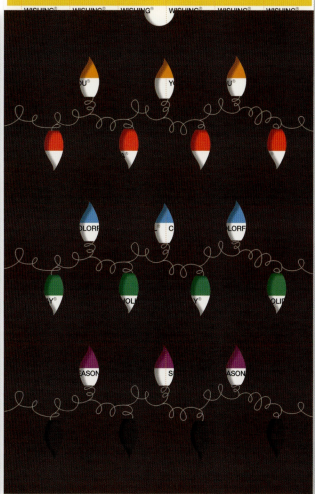

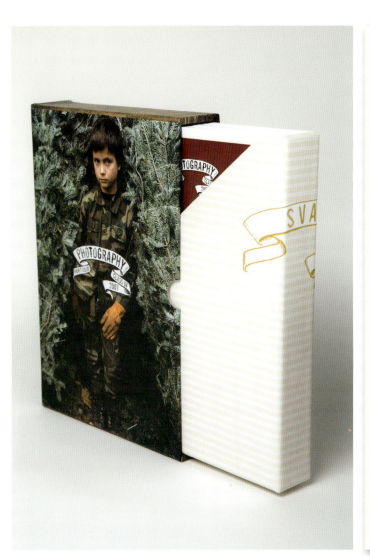

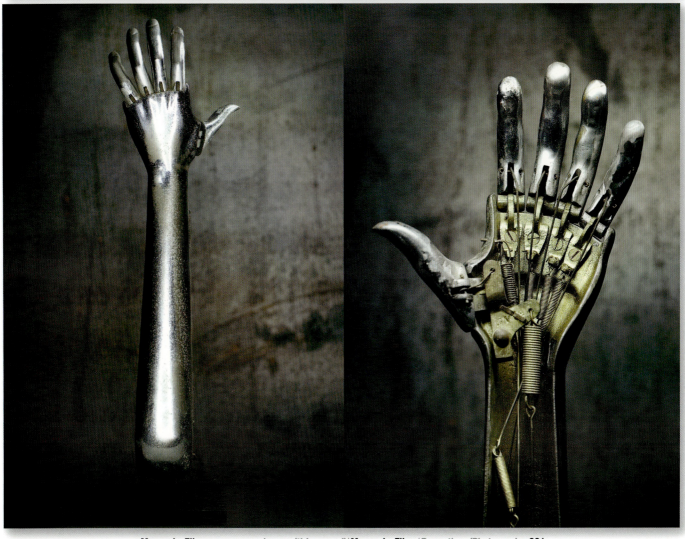

The heartbeat is the universal language of medicine.

71 BPM

St. George's University
THINK BEYOND

Grenada, West Indies

www.sgu.edu

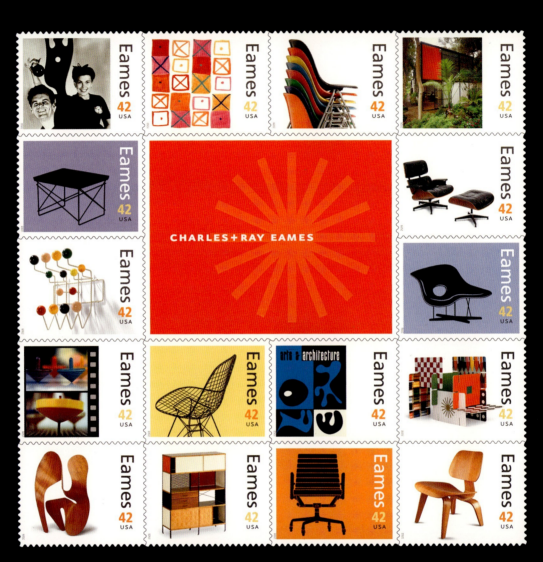

AUSTRALIA SAVE WATER 50c

AUSTRALIA REDUCE WASTE 50c

AUSTRALIA TRAVEL SMART 50c

AUSTRALIA SAVE ENERGY 50c

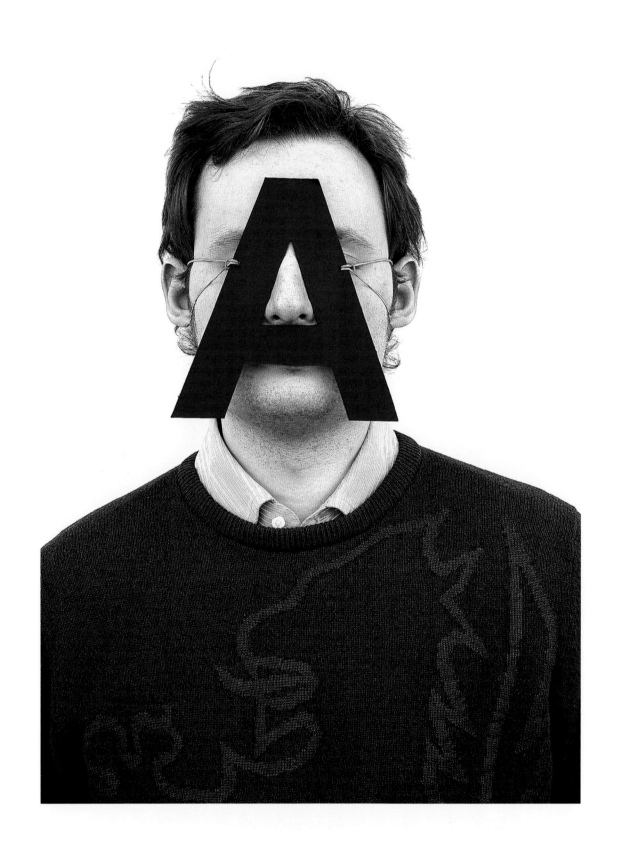

American Face

Chinese Face

Indian Face

Korean Face

Spanish Face

Thai Face

Turkish Face

Japanese Face

ken-tsai lee design studio www.kentsailee.com | Harvest Ads Co., Ltd | Typography234

Credits&Comments

Animation

22 Logo Animation | Design Firm: Venables Bell & Partners, San Francisco | Account Director: Eben Strousse | Art Director: Tavia Holmes | Associate Creative Director: Crockett Jeffers | Chief Creative Officers: Greg Bell, Paul Venables | Design Director, Illustrator, Senior Designer: Blake Bakken | Print Producer: Mike Huntley | Programmer: Cristobal Fernandez | Writer: Nick Cade | Client: Sansa

Description: The logo animation emphasizes the abstraction of the five letters of the word "Sansa" uniquely stacked with the letter "n" centered within the mark to express the playful, energetic personality of the brand.

AnnualReports

23 Annual Report 2007 The Way Things Are | Design Firm: Dietwee communication and design, Utrecht | Account Director: Joost Hosman | Art Director, Creative Director: Tirso Francés | Photographer: Neil Massey | Print Producer: Aukje Spieker | Project Manager: Hein Alkemade | Senior Designer: Jamie Mitchell | Writer: Aquarium Writers London | Client: Bank Insinger de Beaufort

Description: Assignment – Insinger de Beaufort is an Anglo-Dutch private bank and investment house, which likes to stand out from the competition by taking an independent and slightly unconventional approach to finance. Every year the company produces an annual review, which reflects this approach. The Annual Review 2007 is the eighth in a series of diversely themed and designed annual reviews that have the intention to be kept one's bookshelf. It is the challenge to come up with a theme each year that reflects the position, and the view of Insinger de Beaufort on the financial world of the last year. Subsequently the design of the book needs to communicate this seamlessly in a way suitable for a bank. / *Uncertainty* – Uncertainty is the only certainty in today's economy. By acknowledging and acting upon this, Insinger de Beaufort offers added value to its customers. For this year's annual review we went behind the scenes of a leading UK contemporary circus company, NoFit State. Living with uncertainty—knowing their mettle will be tested again and again, but not knowing how—is in the company's DNA. Difficulties are faced and dealt with. A live audience awaits them. The show will go on. In many respects, it would be difficult to find a company that is more different from Insinger de Beaufort than NoFit State. But we did not have to scratch the surface hard to find similar dilemmas and situations confronting us all, on both a human and a corporate level. Thus life in the circus becomes in a way a fitting metaphor. / *Characteristics* – The theme part of this annual review, featuring the NoFit State circus, is divided into five chapters, woven through the CEO statement as a series of 5 book-in-books. By doing this we give, on first level, an impression of the magic show, but inside the book-in-books we get a view into the hectic world behind the show. These hectic circumstances are also portrayed through typography, layout and the photography of Neil Massey, a London based photographer. Typography: Subtle, delicate italic typography for the show text is contrasted with a blunt, bolder layered typography inside the book-in-books. Layout: The full bleed dark imagery of the show, on the large pages, is contrasted with the multilayered images on white pages within the book-in-books, further conveying the contrast between what is seen on the surface and the hectic life within.

24 PLATINUM 2008 Annual Report | Design Firm: WAX, Calgary | Art Director: Jonathan Herman | Creative Directors: Monique Gamache, Joe Hospodarec | Photographer: Justen Lacoursiere | Printer: Blanchette Press | Writer: Saro Ghazarian | Client: Calgary Society for Persons with Disabilities

Description: To express the issue and significance of fundraising on a human level, the entire annual report was written by hand on objects that were purchased from fundraising efforts to help people living with disabilities.

25 Times are Tough | Design Firm: LOWERCASE INC, Chicago | Creative Director, Typographer: Tim Bruce | Designers: Tim Bruce, Emilia Klimiuk | Photographers: Lisa Miller, Tony Armour Photography | Client: Chicago Volunteer Legal Services

26 Annual Report 2007 | Design Firm: Addison, New York | Account Director: Michelle Steg Faranda | Creative Director: Richard Colbourne | Design Director, Designer: Jason Miller | Photographers: Ioulex, Kyoko Hamada, Rick Burda, Burkhard Schittny, Nadav Kander | Print Producer: Georgiann Baran | Typographer: Bernard Maisner | Writer: Robert Roth | Client: Neenah Paper, Inc.

Description: The ultimate goal of the Neenah Paper Annual Report 2007 is simply integration and execution. The report opens with six dramatic, differently designed spreads, each making one strong point: (1) the integration of acquisitions; (2) the company's expansion in premium fine papers; (3) the expansion of "green" papers; (4) growing the global presence; (5) marketing by product lines; and (6) expansion of manufacturing capabilities.

27 Society of Graphic Designers of Canada 2006-07 Annual Report | Design Firm: Bradbury Branding & Design, Regina | Creative Director, Design Director, Designer: Catharine Bradbury | Writer: Kim Ireton | Client: Society of Graphic Designers of Canada

28 Entergy Corporation 2007 Annual Report | Design Firm: Benoit Design, Inc., Plano | Account Director: Alma Benoit | Art Directors: Dennis Benoit, Chuck Hodges | Chief Creative Officer, Creative Director, Creative Strategist, Design Director: Dennis Benoit | Designer: Chuck Hodges | Illustrator: Michael Koelsch | Print Producer: Williamson Printing | Writer: Barbara Kieker | Client: Entergy Corporation

Description: The main objective of the 2007 annual report was to communicate Entergy's ongoing efforts to create, capture and unlock value in its utility and nuclear businesses, and subsequently communicate a great value realization story—a spin-off transaction and its three newly created entities: Entergy Classic, SpinCo and the Nuclear Services Joint Venture.

29 Derwent London plc Report & Accounts 2007 | Design Firm: CDT Design, London | Creative Director: Neil Walker | Designer: Sam Stephens | Project Manager: Alina Abelianova | Senior Designer: Anup Sharma-Yun | Client: Derwent London

Description: Derwent London has developed a strong reputation for anticipating the locations of tomorrow, and contributing to London's regeneration by creating quality working environments for its tenants. The Annual Report was to showcase Derwent's strategy and commitment to design and architecture. The report focuses on the connection between the modern and contemporary art commissioned by Derwent London and the high quality execution that makes their buildings unique. Specially commissioned photography has been used to create a visual story—from the striking art piece cover to the inspired architectural photography inside.

Awards

30 Popcorn box Award | Design Firm: Eduardo del Fraile, Murcia | Creative Director, Designer: Eduardo del Fraile | Client: Movie

Description: Movie is a contest acknowledging the best adverts shown on the big screen. The trophy is a synthesis of the popcorn box. The trophy was not made of metal but of chipboard to give the impression the trophy is similar.

Banners

31 Pentagram Flag | Design Firm: Pentagram, New York | Art Director, Designer: Michael Gericke | Client: Pentagram Design

Description: Pentagram New York office has a long-standing tradition of flying a partner-designed flag outside its Fifth Avenue building. Designed by Michael Gericke, the current flag consists of an interconnected p and d (for Pentagram Design) on a background of Pentagram red.

32 Saint Louis Public Library Banners | Design Firm: TOKY BRANDING + DESIGN, St. Louis | Creative Director: Eric Thoelke | Illustrator: Noah Woods | Senior Designer: Katy Fischer | Client: Saint Louis Public Library Foundation

Books

33 BLOWN | Design Firm: The Auditorium, New York | Creative Directors: Christopher Griffith, Rebecca O'Donnell | Design Director: Rebecca O'Donnell | Photographer: Christopher Griffith | Photographer's Assistant: Eric White | Client: AUDITORIUM Editions

Description: Still life series of blown out tires collected from the highways of the United States.

34 Napa, Behind the Bottle | Design Firm: Hartford Design, Chicago | Art Director, Designer: Tim Hartford | Photographer: Bill Tucker (Photo Retouching - Jeff Tucker) | Print Producer: Hemlock Printers Ltd. | Client: Bill Tucker Studio, Inc.

Description: Napa, Behind the Bottle is a book of portraits of the Napa Valley community of wine makers, owners and the workers who have made the Napa Valley wine industry what it is today. Bill Tucker's photography captures the character of this famous community and the pioneers responsible for some of the world's finest wines. The photographs are memorable, not just a collection of portraits but rather a series of touching, curious, honest, dramatic and sometimes whimsical images. While the elements, the textures, the vines and the barrel rooms influence some of the photographs, the images remain about the people. The heart and soul of the subjects are captured and exposed in a single moment. When you look through these plates the photographs evoke emotions we all share. The passion Bill has for photography mirrors his subjects' passion for making their extraordinary wines. He has brought together for this book the images that most powerfully speak of his personal experiences.

35 PLATINUM Society of Publication Designers Annual 2006 | Design Firm: Jill Greenberg Studio | Creative Directors: Robert Priest, Grace Lee | Photographer: Jill Greenberg | Stylist: Ethan Tobman | Client: Society of Publication Designers

36 (1st) 100 Baseball Icons | Design Firm: Pentagram, San Francisco | Author, Editor: Delphine Hirasuna | Creative Director: Kit Hinrichs | Designers: Kit Hinrichs, Gloria Hiek | Photographer: Terry Heffernan | Client: Ten Speed Press

Description: This book is published by Ten Speed Press in cooperation with the National Baseball Hall of Fame and Museum. It features photographs of baseball artifacts taken by Terry Heffernan at the Hall of Fame archives, with historical background captions written by Delphine Hirasuna. The book is targeted to baseball fans of all ages and people who enjoy beautiful photography and design. It is meant to provide a fun, fascinating, and quick read. This is the first of a series of "100 Icons" books that will be created by Kit Hinrichs, Terry Heffernan and Delphine Hirasuna.

36 (2nd) 100 American Flags | Design Firm: Pentagram, San Francisco | Author, Editor: Delphine Hirasuna | Creative Director: Kit Hinrichs | Designers: Kit Hinrichs, Gloria Hiek | Photographer: Terry Heffernan | Client: Ten Speed Press

Description: "100 American Flags," published by Ten Speed Press, provides a look at how average Americans used and interpreted their nation's banner over the past 230 years. Showcasing the collection of Pentagram designer Kit Hinrichs, the book features 100 sewn, painted, carved, woven, etched, assembled and printed objects displaying the Stars and Stripes. It includes everything from wartime memorabilia and one-of-a-kind artwork to children's toys and Native American beadwork. Photographs were taken by Terry Heffernan and text written by Delphine Hirasuna. This is the second of a series of "100 Icons" books created by Kit Hinrichs, Terry Heffernan and Delphine Hirasuna.

37 Color Chart: Reinventing Color, 1950 To Today | Design Firm: Matsumoto Inc., New York | Art Director, Designer: Takaaki Matsumoto | Client: The Museum of Modern Art

38 No Pictures | Design Firm: Lloyd & Company Advertising, Inc., New York | Account Director: Drazen Kupres | Art Director: Anton Aparin | Creative Director: Douglas Lloyd | Photographer: Ron Galella | Client: Ron Galella

Description: Ron Galella has been regarded as the most controversial photographer of celebrities. For the last 30 years he has given us a pictorial record of the biggest names of the time. 'No Pictures' is his book about confrontations with celebs and shows how unpopular his method often made him with some of his subjects. He didn't invent the word 'paparazzo' but he surely defines it.

39 Naked Ambition | Design Firm: Pentagram Design, Austin | Art Director: DJ Stout | Designer: Daniella Boebel | Client: Michael Grecco

Description: Naked Ambition is "an R rated look at an X rated industry." An exploration of the porn industry through photographs and testimonies.

40 Hum Research Book | Design Firm: Alt Group, Auckland | Creative Director: Dean Poole | Designers: Dean Poole, Shabnam Shiwan, Anna Myers, Aaron Edwards, Tony Proffit, Max Lozach | Photographers: Duncan Cole, Ian Robertson, Toaki Okano, Formway, Alt Group, Kimball Office, Getty Images, Superstock, iStockphoto. Barrett Lyon's Opte Project graphic map of the World Wide Web, http://opte.org/maps http://creativecommons.org/licenses/by/3.0/ | Writers: Dean Poole, David Walker, Pradeep Sharma, Bert Aldridge | Client: Kimball Office / Formway

Description: A research book accompanying the launch of Hum. Minds at Work at Neocon 2008. To provide evidence of the investigation, exploration and design process that led to the development of the product. Furniture has always been designed to fit our bodies. Why hasn't it been designed to fit our minds? To coincide with the launch of Kimball Office and Formway's new product Hum, a book was created to support the research behind the development of the product. The book was designed to function as a tool for facility managers, human resource managers, architects and designers, charged with the task of creating and maintaining high performance workplaces. Its role as a communication piece is to provide evidence of the investigation, exploration and design process that led to the development of the product. This is an entirely pioneering case of evidence-led design. The book builds and amplifies the reputation of the product, and the company bringing it to market.

41 SVA Undergraduate Catalog 2009-2010 | Design Firm: Visual Arts Press, Ltd., New York | Art Director: Michael J. Walsh | Creative Director: Anthony P. Rhodes | Designers: Brian E. Smith, Patrick Tobin, Suck Zoo Han | Client: School of Visual Arts

Description: The goal of the SVA Undergraduate Catalog is to present the capabilities and work of the students at SVA, and highlight everything that is unique about the school, in a way that, we believe, no other school can do. The book aims to prove, undeniably, through factual and visual evidence, that the school is an extraordinary place to study. The catalog has been well received by the SVA community and has been regarded as setting a new standard for publications of its kind.

42 Erik A. Frandsen exhibition book | Design Firm: Punktum design MDD, Copenhagen | Artist: Erik A. Frandsen | Author: Jens Erik Sørensen | Design Director, Designer: Søren Varming | Photographers: Ole Hein and others | Project Manager: Lise Mortensen | Client: ARoS, Aarhus Artmuseum

Description: Exhibition book. ARoS, museum of modern art, Aarhus – Denmark. Erik A. Frandsen exhibition. Erik A. Frandsen is one of the most prominent artists on the contemporary art-scene in Northern Europe. This exhibition is the first retrospective exhibition made of his works from the eighties until now. The design vision for the book was to provide the background beats in a travel through all the transformations that Erik has gone through, since young wild punk-art, through neon, mirrors and rockwool art, until today's finely laid mosaics with snapshot of everyday life. The grid and the choice of Helvetica is made to be a visual background that gives space for the viewer to understand the transformations, without ever taking over the book. On the cover and in the opening pages, we made anagrams of his name to further underline that he is a person consistently on a journey of transformation. The varnish and the silver is to underline that he is a very cool guy, and that his art is actually really cool design! Enjoy the book—we enjoyed making it.

43 DUF/2 | Design Firm: Ontwerphaven, Tilburg | Art Director, Designer: Suzanne Hertogs | Editors: Petra Boers, Suzanne Hertogs, Nicole Ros | Client: Suzanne Hertogs, Ontwerphaven

Description: DUF is an independently published 'bookmazine' created to entice Dutch teenagers to read more. Educational information, no ads, no celebrities (but the teenagers don't experience this as educational, it is all fun and exciting). DUF approaches the teenager in a adult way. Part of DUF is made by teenagers (page 257-280). DUF has a high 'ZAP-factor', with a wide variety of information presented in a playful and exciting manner for youngsters. You can read about sex, science, art, religion, history, food, teenagers difficulties, orgasms, literature... etc! DUF is an adventure; just like reading should be.

44 Extraordinary Lives: Members Since 1958 | Design Firm: VSA Partners, Chicago | Account Director: Lindsey Maino | Creative Director: Hans Neubert | Design Director: Michael Braley | Editor: Peg Tyre | General Director: Alberta Jarane | Print Producer: Lorenz Skeeter | Senior Designer: Jennifer Lee | Client: American Express

Description: This is a limited-edition coffee table book focusing on the lives of 22 featured American Express Charter Cardmembers (those who have had the card since 1958). Each person's unique story was translated by a renowned author and accompanied by distinct illustrations created specifically for the story. This is a collaboration between 22 subjects, 23 writers, and 24 artists from around the world. The artwork shown here was created using a wide range of mediums including watercolors, collage, digital and acrylic. The book was designed in Adobe InDesign CS3.

45 Abundant Australia Book | Design Firm: Frost Design, Sydney | Creative Directors: Vince Frost, Neil Durbach, Wendy Lewin, Gary Warner, Kerstin Thompson | Designers: Joanna Mackenzie, Quan Payne, Frances Ratford, Irmi Wachendorff, Sarah Estens, Natasha Bartosefski, Ben Jennings | Project Manager: Annabel Moir | Client: Royal Australian Institute of Architects

Description: The Venice Biennale is considered to be the most important event in contemporary architecture. Held every two years in Venice, Italy, the Biennale draws influential architects from around the world. This year Vince Frost joined four other creative directors to curate the Australian exhibition. Frost was commissioned by the AIA to create the exhibition identity, logo, and collateral (including brochures, invites, bags, badges, pins and T-shirts) responding to Biennale Director Aaron Betsky's theme: 'Out There: Architecture Beyond Building'. The use of multiple discs in the design references the natural, structural and experimental forms used by architects. Vibrant yellow is strongly featured in the exhibition environment as well as on print and collateral, creating a fun, fresh design that evokes a sense of lively 'Australian-ness'. He was also commissioned to create a catalogue that would display the 300 models that were contributed to the exhibition. Incorporating the multiple discs used in the other collateral, the catalogue takes on its own experimental form. It includes an academic essay that provides an historical context for the models and the future ideas displayed in the exhibition. The catalogue served as a reference for visitors to the Biennale but it has a lifespan beyond the exhibition.

46 (top left) The Film Club | Design Firm: The DesignWorks Group, Sisters | Author: David Gilmore | Creative Director: Anne Twomey | Designer: Tim Green | Client: Grand Central Publishing

46 (top right) Miss Fortune | Design Firm: The DesignWorks Group, Sisters | Author: Sara Mills | Creative Director: Judy Tollberg | Designer: Charles Brock | Client: Moody Publishers

46 (bottom left) Doghead | Design Firm: St. Martin's Press, New York | Art Director, Creative Director, Designer: Steve Snider | Client: St. Martin's Press

46 (bottom right) THE 351 BOOKS OF IRMA ARCURI | Design Firm: Penguin Group (USA) Inc., New York | Art Director, Designer: Paul Buckley | Photographer: Fredrik Broden | Client: Penguin Group (USA) Inc., New York

47 The New Annotated Dracula | Design Firm: The DesignWorks Group, Sisters | Author: Bram Stoker | Creative Director: Eleen Cheung | Designer, Typographer: Charles Brock | Client: WW Norton

48 Zibaldone de las Cinco Etapas de la Vida | Design Firm: Ana Cortils Comunicacion Visual, Madrid | Art Director, Author, Designer: Ana Cortils | Editor: TF: Editores | Photographers: Ana Cortils & others (collage) | Print Producer: TF. Artes Graficas, Cromotex | Client: TF Artes Graficas

Description: "Zibaldone de las Cinco Etapas de la Vida" (Diary of the Five Stages of Life: Five Times Nine Visual Haikus). Outline of a book project for an exclusive printing company on the occasion of its 20th anniversary. TF. is also a publishing company for art books.

Principle objectives – To create a book concerning the different stages and aspects of human life. To bring together collage, fonts, photography and ancient Chinese and Japanese cultures. / *Zibaldone (concept)* – Italian for "scrapbook," as in the famous "Zibaldone of Leopardi." / *Chinese Charts (index reference)* – the objective was to resume—using the organizing principle of the Five Stages of Human Life—all of the principle constitutive concepts of each, grouped according to color, the seasons of the year, cardinal directions, senses, emotions, psychological states or values, flavors, etc. Each stage of life corresponds to a cardinal direction or point, as well as a particular emotion, psychological state, etc. For the book, nine groups, each with its corresponding 5 stages, were chosen, for a total of 45 compositions or visual concepts. / *Visual haikus* – As in the case of verbal haiku, the idea is to achieve maximum communication with the fewest possible elements, thus allowing each viewer to "finish the [visual] sentence" according to his or her personal experience. / *Desired Result* – A subtle book which invites the viewer to reflect on life, one which might serve to inspire meditation. On the other hand, it is important that the book be elegant and unusual, and that it exhibit the client's printing skills and capacities to the best effect possible (TF. is considered one of Spain's finest printing companies), but without ostentation. / *Inspiration* – Principally the philosophy and art of Zen, although by its very nature a scrapbook, and one whose principal theme is life itself, could not be other than eclectic. Another source of inspiration was found in medieval "Books of Hours." / *Languages* – Spanish, English and Chinese (the English translation is found at the end of the book). Chinese characters are used only in the titles of each stage, and in those of each image. / *Printing Details* – Two different kinds of Italian papers, Old Mill for text pages, and Phoenix Xantur for images pages. / *Inks* – 15 spot colors in some sections and 4 different kinds of varnish. Cover: Hardcover with dust jacket and shell case.

49 Practicing | Design Firm: Peter Mendelsund Design | Art Director: Carol Devine Carson | Designer: Peter Mendelsund | Photographer: Glenn Kurtz | Client: Alfred A. Knopf

Branding

50, 51 Rebecca Beeson Identity | Design Firm: Rob Duncan Design, San Francisco | Creative Director, Designer: Rob Duncan | Client: Rebecca Beeson

Description: Identity system for a fashion designer.

52, 53 Okanagan Spring Brewery Brand Identity System | Design Firm: Subplot Design Inc., Vancouver | Art Director, Designer, Illustrator, Typographer: Matthew Clark | Creative Directors, Creative Strategists, Design Directors: Matthew Clark, Roy White | Photographer: Clinton Hussey | Writers: Matthew Clark, Jeff Lewis | Client: Okanagan Spring Brewery

Description: Okanagan Spring Brewery Brand Identity System. In its first 20 years, Okanagan Spring had grown to become British Columbia's leading craft beer brand. Despite top marks for the liquid itself, the brand had low recall, poor differentiation, and had no unaided recall even among diehard fans. The objective was to reposition the brand and reinforce the all-natural, handcrafted positioning and emphasize their craft-brewing expertise.

54, 55 Branding / Hotel Identity System | Design Firm: IMAGE: Global Vision, Santa Monica | Creative Director: Regina Rubino | Design Directors: Regina Rubino, Robert Louey | Designers: Emily Carlson, Javier Leguizamo, Claudia Pandji | Photographers: Karyn Millet, Corey Weiner | Print Producer: Clear Image Printing, Katercraft, Misc. | Client: The Grand Del Mar

Description: Brand Identity for Mediterranean Estate Hotel including custom made leather box compendium with hand made Italian paper liners, guest folio, key cards, postcards, book marks, seed packet turn down amenity, banquet tags, coffee cups, water bottle labels, pool menu, spa packaging signage and golf score cards, yardbooks and promotional/sales items.

56, 57 NetApp - Creating a gateway to opportunities | Design Firm: Landor Associates, San Francisco | Account Director: Emily Miller | Creative Director: JJ Ha | Executive Creative Director: Nicolas Apparicio | Executive Director: Deborah Crudo | Project Manager: Mignon Monroe | Senior Designers: Ivan Thelin, Michael Lin, Henri Kusbiantoro | Client: NetApp

Description: NetApp (formerly known as Network Appliance) is a world leader in unified storage solutions for data-intensive enterprises. Since its inception in 1992, NetApp has delivered technology, product, and partner firsts that simplify data management. NetApp started off as a small start-up company and garnered extraordinary success. Despite its achievements, it retained an entrepreneurial environment. Its storage solutions include specialized hardware, software, and services that provide storage management for open network environments. NetApp's technically minded customers, partners, and employees were fiercely devoted to its products but it wanted to expand its role from a niche storage solutions player to a strategic global IT partner. To do that, NetApp needed to connect with a critical new audience—strategic decision makers and executives—while remaining relevant to its core technical devotees. NetApp wanted to create awareness at the C-suite level and convince these executives it was a trustworthy company, and more than just a start-up. Preserving NetApps' existing equities including relentless innovation, first-rate technology, and a customer-centric culture was also crucial to its growth. Landor conducted extensive consumer research with current, potential, and competitor's customers and concluded that NetApp was widely perceived as having superior technology and incredible customer service. Landor created the Brand Driver™ go beyond to reinforce NetApp's commitment to "do whatever it takes." We also recommended it adopt NetApp as it's official corporate name. To communicate its desire for a strong human connection—a unique promise in the B2B and technology categories—we introduced a warmer visual identity and photo style. Landor developed fresh messaging, including a new, humanistic brandline that was more responsive to NetApp's customers.

58, 59 Luckyfish Identity Program | Design Firm: Pentagram, San Francisco | Creative Director: Kit Hinrichs | Senior Designer: Laura Scott | Client: Luckyfish

Description: Kit Hinrichs and Laura Scott have designed the identity for Luckyfish, a new sushi restaurant in Beverly Hills by Innovative Dining, the Los Angeles-based restaurant group that also operates the popular Sushi Roku, BOA Steakhouse and Katana. Hip in ambience and mid-range in price, Luckyfish reinterprets and elevates the traditional kaiten-zushi (conveyor-belt style sushi) experience. A visual translation of the name, the Luckyfish logo highlights one of eight fish in red, the color for good luck in Japanese culture, and references the restaurant's conveyor belt service. The identity is used comprehensively throughout all the restaurant's graphics, extending to signage, the website, menus and dinnerware as well as T-shirts, baseball caps and other ancillary items. To reinforce the fun nature of the brand, the theme of good luck was threaded throughout the communications system. Humorous quotes with the word lucky in them were printed on the backs of bartender t-shirts and at the bottoms of take-out boxes. Take-away gifts, custom scratch-offs and fortune fish were also designed to keep guests entertained.

60, 61 Homebase Instore Branding & Point of Sale | Design Firm: Turner Duckworth, CA | Creative Directors: David Turner, Bruce Duckworth | Designers: Charlotte Barres, Christian Eager, Dave Germain, Mike Harris, Gavin Hurrell, Jamie McCathie, Mark Waters | Editors: Matt Hall, Peter Ruane | Illustrator: Peter Ruane | Photographer: Phil Cooke | Print Producer: Alistair Porchetta | Client: Homebase Ltd

Description: Homebase approached Turner Duckworth to revitalize the in-store branding across their retail estate. The aim was to make finding Homebase products easier, while providing advice and inspiration at point of purchase. The result is a navigation system that makes finding what you came for easy and fun, pointing out tips and alternatives along the way; the simple, clean graphics mean you will never be lost down the wrong aisle again!

62, 63 Office Games | Design Firm: The Partners, London | Creative Director: Jack Renwick | Designers: Samuel Hall, Alex Woolley, Neil Southwell | Illustrator: Alex Woolley | Photographers: Samuel Hall, Dave Wood | Client: Richard House Children's Hospice

Description: Context – Richard House Children's Hospice is a charity that helps make life easier for terminally ill children and their families. They hold various fundraisers throughout the year and had organized a new July event at Broadgate Arena. 'Office Games' brings together both office and sport to create a unique contest. *Events include:* Floppy Discus, Office Chair Relay, Recycling Rowing, and Post-it Note Fencing. / *Brief* – Richard House needed a logo and visual language that would excite people for the fundraiser's pilot year and lay the foundations for a strong identity for future events. They didn't want it to appear too "charity-like" and overtly guilt people into taking part. They wanted the focus to be on the fun and enjoyment of the event. / *The Solution* – The humble paperclip became the heart of the identity, creating the main running track logo and a set of icons depicting each sporting event. Marketing communications included banners, flyers, animations, posters and T-shirts. Bold use of the core red gave us a cost effective way of achieving maximum impact.

Brochures

64 Student Prospectus | Design Firm: North Charles Street Design Organization, Baltimore | Account Director: Susan Repko | Art Director: Courtney Lausch | Creative Director: Bernice Thieblot | Photographer: Don Hamerman | Writer: Matthew Westbrook | Client: The University of the South (Sewanee)

Description: The prospectus seeks to forge a wider appreciation for the extraordinary opportunities offered by the University. A record of 25 Rhodes Scholars, for example, testifies to its capacity to nurture talent. Its 13,000-acre campus, which incorporates the town of Sewanee, is not only a laboratory for environmental study and a site for recreation, but also home to the entire college community in which each student can play a vital role. The piece is sent upon request to high school students.

65 PLATINUM Centropolis Design corporate brochure | Design Firm: Cacao Design, Milano | Author: Cacao Design creative staff | Creative Directors: Mauro Pastore, Masa Magnoni, Alessandro Floridia | Typographer: Fontegrafica | Client: Centropolis Design

Description: Corporate brochure designed for Centropolis Design, an interior design company specialized in luxury design. By a harmonic fusion of different materials (paper, laked wood, textile, aluminum), the brochure itself becomes an interior design object, a real decor complement.

66, 67 Born to Print | Design Firm: Squires & Company, Dallas | Art Director: Brandon Murphy | Artist: Ernesto Pacheco | Associate Creative Director: Bret Sano | Designers: Justin King, Bret Sano | Writer: Wayne Geyer | Photographer: Michael Lichter | Client: Domtar Paper

Description: The Born to Print promotional piece was intended to promote Domtar Lynx paper as the go-to house sheet for printers and so it was important to design a piece that would show off the printing capabilities of the paper while speaking to the target audience.

68 Ingo Schulze: My Second Coat | Design Firm: ANDRE GRAU, LEIPZIG | Author: Ingo Schulze | Art Director, Designer, Typographer: Andre Grau | Editor: Leipziger Bibliophilen-Abend e.V. | Project Manager: Herbert Kaestner | Client: Leipziger Bibliophilen-Abend e.V.

Description: Includes a signed original woodcut print by Hartwig Ebersbach. A group of German writers is drawn into a literary publicity tour through China. Unexpectedly, author Ingo Schulze experiences 33 moments of luck that lead him to the surprising discovery of his "second coat". The concertina folder was published by the Leipziger Bibliophilen-Abend e.V. association as part of the "StichWORT" series, an edition of unpublished texts by contemporary writers.

69 Multiplex Living settlement kit | Design Firm: Hoyne Design, St Kilda | Creative Director: Dan Johnson | Designers: Dan Johnson, Felicity Davison | Photographer: Marcus Struzina | Client: Multiplex Living

Description: This pack is presented to all purchasers of Multiplex property. The kit contains a range of details including warranties, local amenities and strata information. A stylish look and feel ensures that each kit has an ornamental rather than functional quality that encourages purchasers to place them prominently on display in their homes.

70 Brochure | Design Firm: Tomorrow Partners, Berkeley | Designer: Monica Hernandez | Executive Creative Director: Gaby Brink | Client: Scharffen Berger

Description: The Scharffen Berger brochure, elegantly shaped like one of the company's signature bars, features evocative close-ups of both product and process.

71 Otis College of Art and Design Undergraduate Viewbook | Design Firm: ALT Design, Los Angeles | Art Directors, Designers: Jessica Fleischmann, Ana Llorente | Client: Otis College of Art and Design

Description: The 2008-2009 Otis Viewbook is the undergraduate admissions catalog for Otis College of Art and Design, a small, independent art school with a long history in Los Angeles, California. The goal of this 116-page, 4-color recruitment catalog is to invite potential students to visit the campus by presenting the school as a friendly, supportive, diverse environment where students receive professional, world-class training in art and design. Two designers with independent studios came together to collaborate on this project. After extensive research and conceptual development, we decided to put the students and their work in the forefront by minimizing our "hand" as designers, all the while retaining a considered, lively presence. Our main goal was to make an immersive Viewbook—a sort of virtual tour of Otis—as well as to provide a forum in which students speak to their future peers while still clearly presenting the administration's vision. Structurally, the Viewbook organizes information with two distinct coding systems. The first system utilizes brightly colored lozenges at the top edge of the page to indicate the program in which the work on that page was made. (The colors identifying each program are predetermined by the school's identity.) In the second coding system, quarter-circles on the lower left corners progress from white through grey to black, and indicate nine sections or chapters. Each section has its own visual language: from the image-saturated and student quote-rich "who we are," to the type-only "what we study", from the mash-up of photos of student life, quotes, and work in "OTISLAND," to the image only gallery of student work in "what we make II". Three-quarters through the project our print budget was slashed, cutting pages and taking away most of the bells-and-whistles we had planned (multiple paper stocks, scratch-off ink, glow-in-the-dark ink). This challenged us to tighten design moves. With one paper stock and 4-color process throughout, we focused the section shifts on typography and grids. We were able to incorporate one "value added" bonus, a 3-color split fountain poster with admissions info on one side and a "sketch O" (an interpretation of the Otis "O" logo made up of a variety of student sketches) on the other. This comes in two colorways, adding to the collectability of the poster. We were also able to print an additional 500 single-sided posters of the "sketch O" for the development office's use. This is the first Otis Viewbook to thoroughly feature student work and the collective nature of student life at Otis. We went far beyond the original project brief which asked the designer to give form to provided texts and images. Rather, we chose to act as content providers and solicit, generate, and curate a large body of student work and documentary imagery. We closely observed the life of the school in order to accurately and sensitively present the richness and exuberance of student work and life at Otis, an exuberance that begins on the spine, with a declaration by a student. We were closely involved in photography, attending and directing most photo shoots and taking pictures ourselves. We knew that an "above-and-beyond-our-standards" end result would depend on:—Our full involvement in all aspects of the project, including content development, rather than only utilizing materials provided by the client.—During the research phase of the project, we performed an extensive survey of major US art-school catalogs which left us underwhelmed. These catalogs ranged from the corporate to the intellectual, but few stood out as tactile, emotional pieces that invite the 17 to 20-year-old target audience to explore the school from afar. Our catalog does this!—Vibrant, tactile storytelling that inspires potential students to visit Otis became our grail after this survey. Every page is a small world, every spread matters. Each section reveals the richness of studying art at Otis through the eyes and the work of students.—This copy is Year Two, with a bright, compelling new cover which spotlights a student painting. Several spreads have been updated with new photography.—This year, for the first time ever, Otis has a waiting list. We believe this is an indication of the success of Year One in speaking to our target audience.

72, 73 Brochure | Design Firm: Foundry Creative, Calgary | Creative Director: Alison Wattie | Designer: Kylie Henry | Photographer: Ric Kokotovich | Client: Hannon Richards Architecture

Description: As artists, we drool over any kind of creative endeavor that is pure and uncompromised. So naturally we were beside ourselves with the chance to do some work for Hannon Richards. We can only imagine how the people actually buying the homes feel.

74, 75 Tragon Capabilities Brochure | Design Firm: Pentagram, San Francisco | Author: Kirsten Bickford | Creative Director: Kit Hinrichs | Designers: Kit Hinrichs, Erica Wilcott | Photographer: Terry Heffernan | Client: Tragon Corporation

Description: Pentagram designed a new capabilities brochure for Tragon, a world leader in sensory evaluation research. Tragon is an expert at insightfully quantifying highly qualitative categories. Tragon wanted to introduce their new identity and capabilities to existing clients and new prospects, become more visible to the marketing departments, rather than just the research departments, and showcase both the breadth and depth of their capabilities through insightful case study examples.

76 Brand Book | Design Firm: Colle + McVoy | Client: Field and Stream

77 Brochure | Design Firm: MiresBall, San Diego | Account Director: Kristi Jones | Creative Director: Scott Mires | Designer: Dylan Jones | Client: Vulcan Motor Club

Description: Vulcan Motor Club offers its members—predominantly high-net-worth men—access to some of the most luxurious, high-performance cars in the world. This piece is designed to help drive membership. It is intended to be a piece that would be kept over time, and draw you back to the web site to join the club. This brochure is designed to appeal to both the sensual and masculine experience of driving a luxury automobile, along with the pragmatic aspects of owning such a vehicle. A seductive photography style shows just enough car to engage the imagination while a detailed narrative highlights the exhilaration of driving a high-performance car and the practical advantages of club membership—convenience, cost-savings and flexibility.

Calendars

78, 79 PLATINUM WALL | Design Firm: Landor Associates, Sydney | Art Directors: Jason Little, Joao Peres, Ivana Martinovic, Sam Pemberton | Creative Director: Jason Little | Executive Creative Director: Mike Staniford | Designers, Illustrators, Typographers: Jason Little, Ivana Martinovic, Sam Pemberton, Joao Peres | Photographers: Adrian Lander, Michael Hall, Karl Schwerdtfeger, James Cant | Print Producer: Macdonald & Masterson | Writer: Claire Crethar | Client: Spicers Paper

Description: Each year Spicers Paper likes to send out a calendar as a piece of design that not only promotes different papers throughout the year, but equally expresses its commitment to the design industry in Australia.

Whether in the name of beauty, nostalgia or practicality, the items we display on our four walls say something about each and every one of us. Seen through the eyes of four designers and four photographers, WALL pays homage to these wall displays, whilst reflecting each season of the year.

80 Igepa Calendar 2009 | Design Firm: Bruketa&Zinic OM, Zagreb | Account Director: Goran Paleka | Art Director, Designer: Tomislav Jurica Kacunic | Creative Directors: Davor Bruketa, Nikola Zinic | Typographers: Joel Nordstrom, Nikola Djurek | Client: Igepa Plana Papers

Description: This is a non-print calendar for Igepa Plana Papers, a distributor of graphic and office papers. The assignment was to make a calendar for their clients that could at the same time promote their skin paper series. It is a very exquisite and expensive paper they produce in 12 different shades. The idea was to make a calendar like a catalogue with paper samples that Igepa Plana Papers usually uses. The calendar is laser cut, nothing is printed, so the structure of the paper can be perceived even better, and the graphism between different paper colors is intensified.

81 Corporative Calendar Direct Design Visual Branding | Design Firm: Design Works | Creative Director: D. Peryshkov, L. Feygin | Client: Direct Design Visual Branding

Description: Day after day. Month after month. 365 days. But we live only in those days which we remember. Many days fly by without a trace. To tear off a leaf with number. To remember and write down the brightest. The exciting. To lower in a coin box of the brightest days. On December 31st to look and recollect how many bright days you have lived in this year.

82 Planet Art | Design Firm: Studio Joseph Jibri, Tel Aviv | Account Director: David Arnon | Art Director, Creative Director, Creative Strategist, Design Director: Joseph Jibri | Designer: Noam Shidlowsky | Editor: David Arnon | Project Managers: David Arnon, Joseph Jibri | Client: Matan Arts Publishers Ltd.

Description: Planet Art calendar reflects the love of nature from the beginning of mankind, offers artistic combinations of photographs, design and computer graphic, using various printing technologies.

83 Emerson, Wajdowicz Studios 2009 Agenda Calendar | Design Firm: Emerson, Wajdowicz Studios, New York | Art Directors, Creative Directors: Jurek Wajdowicz, Lisa LaRochelle | Designers: Lisa LaRochelle, Yoko Yoshida, Jurek Wajdowicz, Manny Mendez | Photographer: Jurek Wajdowicz | Client: Emerson, Wajdowicz Studios

Description: 2009 Agenda Calendar created by Emerson, Wajdowicz Studios.

Catalogues

84, 85 PLATINUM The Collaborative Art Catalogue | Design Firm: The Partners, London | Creative Director: Nick Eagleton | Designers: Emily Picot, Joe Russell | Photographer: Joe Russell | Client: The Jerwood Space

Description: Objective – Design a catalogue to accompany an exhibition about the process of collaborative art. / *Concept* – Each visitor gets a huge printed sheet and some simple instructions for cutting, folding and binding. The audience performs the final act of collaboration by producing the exhibition catalogue themselves. / *Result* – 1000 sheets, 1000 unique catalogues.

86 2009 Custom Vehicle Operations Motorcycles | Design Firm: VSA Partners, Chicago | Account Director: Melissa Schwister | Creative Director: Dana Arnett | Design Director: Luke Galambos | Designer: Dave Hanicak | Photographer: Midcoast Studios | Writer: Joe Grimberg | Client: Harley-Davidson

87 SIEGER Collection | Design Firm: Novita Communications, Brooklyn | Client: SIEGER Collection

Description: Multiple marketing/promotional materials to support the SIEGER Collection of luxury home and fashion accessories.

88, 89 Lida Baday Fall 2008 Brochure | Design Firm: Concrete Design Communication, Toronto | Art Directors: Diti Katona, John Pylypczak | Designer: Agnes Wong | Photographer: Chris Nicholls | Client: Lida Baday

Description: Lida Baday Fall 2008. Hyper-seductive photography, dramatic understatement and simple but calculated pacing are the hallmarks of the Lida Baday Spring 2008 Collection brochure. With offices in Toronto and New York, Lida Baday designs and produces well-detailed, beautiful clothing that capture the essence of thoughtful, discerning, modern women. The brochure uses clothing, not for the purposes of documentation, but as an expression of the woman who is intelligent, feminine, confident and ultimately modern.

90 Il Bianco Lino E Il Nero | Design Firm: Methodologie, Seattle | Account Director, Creative Director: Anne Traver | Designer: Goretti Kao | Editor: Paula Thurman | Photographer: Russell Johnson | Print Producer: Dave Brass | Project Manager: Mary Weisnewski | Client: Traver Gallery

91 Contrast in Harmony | Design Firm: Vanderbyl Design, San Francisco | Art Director, Designer: Michael Vanderbyl | Photographer: Widner Photography | Client: HBF

92 SIEGER Collection | Design Firm: Novita Communications, Brooklyn | Client: SIEGER Collection

Description: Multiple marketing/promotional materials to support the SIEGER Collection of luxury home and fashion accessories.

93 C Collection by Yves Behar for HBF | Design Firm: Vanderbyl Design, San Francisco | Art Director, Designer: Michael Vanderbyl | Photographer: Widner Photography | Client: HBF

94, 95 new editions | Design Firm: Beierarbeit, Bielefeld | Account Director: Klaus Seebode | Creative Director: Christoph Beier | Designer: André Nickels | Photographer: Christian R. Schulz | Project Manager: Julia Grimm | Web Developer: Thomas Fiedler | Client: Hans Kaufeld

Description: A promotion catalogue for the international furniture trade fair in Cologne 2009. Positioning of the brand Hans Kaufeld as an exquisite and design driven company as a competitor to the Italian leading brand. The publication wants to create a feeling of German precision in combination with sophisticated high-class design—a superior product.

DVDs

96 Casablanca - Ultimate Collector's Edition DVD | Design Firm: 30sixty Advertising+Design, Inc., Studio City | Creative Director: Pär Larsson | Executive Creative Director: Henry Vizcarra | Client: Warner Home Video

Description: Designed to give fans a taste of the romantic, exotic adventure that is Casablanca, this multi-disc DVD Ultimate Collector's Edition is detailed with a Moorish design and color palette that's integrated in the stylish laser-cut o-sleeve. From the collectible photo book, complete with insightful, behind-the-scenes information on the creation of this timeless film, to the leather luggage I.D. tags and passport holder to the reproduction lobby cards and theatrical key art post cards, this gift set is certain to fulfill everyone's demand for this one-of-a-kind film classic.

97 Mashima: A Life in Four Chapters | Design Firm: Kellerhouse, Inc., Topanga | Art Directors: Neil Kellerhouse, Sarah Habibi | Creative Director, Design Director, Designer, Illustrator, Typographer: Neil Kellerhouse | Client: The Criterion Collection

Description: Slip case, 8-panel digi, two discs, and a 60 page book.

Paul Schrader's visually stunning, collage-like portrait of acclaimed Japanese author and playwright Yukio Mishima (played by Ken Ogata) investigates the inner turmoil and contradictions of a man who attempted an impossible harmony between self, art, and society. Taking place on Mishima's last day, when he famously committed public seppuku, the film is punctuated by extended flashbacks to the writer's life as well as by gloriously stylized evocations of his fictional works. With its rich cinematography by John Bailey, exquisite sets and costumes by Eiko Ishioka, and unforgettable, highly influential score by Philip Glass, Mishima: A Life in Four Chapters is a tribute to its subject and a bold, investigative work of art in its own right.

Editorial

98, 99 Fall Winter 2008/2009: The Shoes Issue | Design Firm: Tank Design, Cambridge | Creative Director, Editor: Mary Talato | Designer: Brian Thomas | Project Manager: Jaclyn Alderete-Cerrato | Senior Designer: Steve Rura | Stylist: Masayo Kishi | Client: Camouflage Magazine

Description: With a talented set of international contributors, the bi-annual publication is a diverse collection of design, photography and editorial, drawing together contemporary with vintage to create its own unique look. The inaugural issue of Camouflage Magazine is all about the world's fascination with Shoes and includes interviews and work from Austrian-born photographer Bela Borsod, illustrator Stine Persson, and shoe designer Charlotte Dellal with a special feature on model Alice Dellal. Camouflage Magazine is distributed in the US, UK, Canada, France, Australia. The Fall 2008 Shoes Issue hit select book stores late October 2008.

100 FLAUNT | Design Firm: FLAUNT | Designer: RGB6 | Photographer: Kalle dos Santos | Client: FLAUNT

101 FLAUNT | Design Firm: FLAUNT | Artist: Hisham Bharoocha | Client: FLAUNT

102 (1st) The Sweet Science of Swimsuits, (2nd) An Oral History of Rudy Giuliani's Temper | Design Firm: GQ, New York | Design Director: Fred Woodward | Client: GQ

103 (1st) Violence of the Lambs, (2nd) World Without Oil | Design Firm: GQ, New York | Design Director: Fred Woodward | Client: GQ

104, 105 Ampersand | Design Firm: Frost Design, Sydney | Creative Director: Vince Frost | Design Director: Anthony Donovan | Designer: Adrian Hing | Writer: Lakshmi Bhaskaran | Client: D&AD

Description: D&AD is an educational charity with a purpose to set creative standards, educate, inspire and promote good design and advertising. Ampersand is also a magazine obsessed by ideas. The Ampersand name came about for a number of reasons. First it was at the heart of the D&AD logo. Secondly it expressed connection—the glue that could hold an infinite diversity of content together. Lastly, within a masthead, the ampersand could portray the home of all great ideas—the thought bubble. Typographically, the issues take a dramatic turn, utilising a custom-engineered typeface with a key difference—the ability to form a third dimension, with interlocking ascenders and descenders, symbolic of the 3D nature of the digital medium. Ampersand Digital looks at how digital design is one of the fastest and evolving fields within the creative industries. These 2 issues focus on the latest developments and talks to the many rising stars of the digital world. The Awards Issue is created to coincide with the D&AD awards celebrating the year's most inspiring creativity. This issue is the last in the digital volume, and uses Ampersand's bold, graphic approach to provide a showcase for the featured work.

106 Clear Magazine | Design Firm: Clear Magazine, Sterling Heights | Client: Clear Magazine

Description: Clear Magazine announces the publication of its first tree-less, 100 percent recyclable magazine. Printed on YUPO© synthetic papers, Clear's latest issue, themed "fame underground," will premiere at December's Design Miami/Basel festival, where Clear is also a media partner. This environmentally friendly publication is the brainchild of Clear founder and creative director Emin Kadi. Clear's unique, limited edition "green" solution closes the gap on source reduction and recycling. YUPO© is completely waterproof, stain resistant and very durable. Its unique printing surface results in exceptional color reproduction and print clarity. YUPO© is a perfect match for Clear, which has always been special and collectable. Clear's November/December issue will withstand the wear and tear of the repeated viewing that it demands. YUPO© papers' light weight allows significant fuel reduction in shipping and a lower overall carbon footprint. Should one wish to dispose of the issue, it may be placed in a recycling bin with any other plastic items, and it will be fully recycled. "Our goal is to provide readers with stunning presentations of the world's most interesting and creative artists and events. Our new partnership with Yupo allows us to do so in an environmentally responsible, respectful way. Design Miami/Basel is the perfect occasion to share our green accomplishment," says publisher Emin Kadi. YUPO© is a 100% "tree-free" product, containing neither timber nor any other organic fiber. As such, YUPO© contributes to the preservation of our natural timber

resources. YUPO© synthetic paper generates no detectable amounts of sulfur, chlorine, nitrogen, or dioxin gases when properly incinerated and generates less heat energy compared to other plastics. No ozone layer threatening emissions result from the manufacturing process. 100% Recyclable YUPO© synthetic paper is a category 5 polypropylene (PP) plastic film.

About Clear Magazine – By lending intuitive editorial with clever, cutting-edge design, Clear Magazine enhances the mind while satisfying the visual senses of today's informed reader. Clear is the ultimate curator of interesting items, objects and ideas in the world of design, fashion and art. Visually unique and intriguing, Clear successfully bridges the gap between the indie and the classic publication. In short, Clear is today's ultimate international medium that caters to all the senses.

107 Prefix Photo 18 | Design Firm: Underline Studio, Toronto | Art Directors: Claire Dawson, Fidel Pena, Scott McLeod | Designer: Emily Tu | Editor: Scott McLeod | Client: Prefix Institute of Contemporary Art

Description: Prefix Photo is an engaging magazine that presents contemporary Canadian photography in an international context. Characterized by innovative design and outstanding production values, it features photography portfolios and critical essays.

108-111 Dear Dave, Issue #3 | Design Firm: Visual Arts Press, Ltd., New York | Art Director, Designer: Michael J. Walsh | Creative Director: Anthony P. Rhodes | Client: School of Visual Arts

Description: Dear Dave is a photography magazine published twice a year by the BFA Photography Department and is sold in stores.

Environmental

112, 113 American Express Asia Pacific Headquarters | Design Firm: Frost Design, Sydney | Creative Director: Vince Frost | Design Director: Carlo Giannasca | Designer: Siobhan Murphy | Project Manager: Annabel Moir | Client: American Express Asia Pacific

Description: American Express approached us to develop global branding graphics for their new Asia-Pacific Headquarters in Sydney. The resulting environmental graphics includes floor to ceiling wallpaper created with black and white photographs by Annie Leibovitz, room identification inspired by credit card numbering and graphics literally made up from the brand value text, a kind of hidden brand mantra. The environmental graphics cover all 11-storeys of the new building located at King Street Wharf and reinforce the global branding, whilst giving staff an engaging and attractive environment to work in.

114 Syracuse University/S. I. Newhouse School of Public Communications Atrium Mural | Design Firm: Poulin + Morris Inc., New York | Creative Director: Richard Poulin | Designers: Richard Poulin, Brian Brindisi, Alpkan Kirayoglu | Client: Polshek Partnership Architects

Description: Poulin + Morris was commissioned by Polshek Partnership Architects to develop an overall environmental graphics and donor recognition sign program to link the various areas of Newhouse III, the latest building in the S. I. Newhouse School of Public Communications complex. The visual solutions implemented rely upon the use of visual metaphor and technology to communicate the foundation and future mission of this premiere school of journalism. A typographic wall mural located in the "heart" or atrium of the new building spans three stories identifying "NEWHOUSE" and its programs such as media studies, journalism, and graphic design. By using CMYK-colored halftone dots, Poulin + Morris created a visual metaphor celebrating "NEWHOUSE" and its pursuits of traditional and non-traditional forms of public communications in the new digital era. Poulin + Morris' dynamic visual solutions function as meaningful and memorable symbols for the School. The solutions needed to be rich and engaging; not only to inspire, but to connect with the spirit, energy, diversity, professionalism, and creativity of past, present, and future generations.

115 Luminary | Design Firm: Y&L / 2nd Globe, Indianapolis | Artist: Jeff Laramore | Location: Indiana University Melvin and Bren Simon Cancer Center | Photographer: Tod Martens | Client: IU Cancer Center

116, 117 California Academy of Sciences Museum | Design Firm: Volume Inc., San Francisco | Creative Directors: Adam Brodsley, Eric Heiman | Designers: Margot Piper, Iran Narges, Talin Wadsworth | Executive Directors: Jonathan Katz, Cinnabar Inc. (Executive Producer) | Project Managers: Jeannie Lomma, Cinnabar Inc. | Senior Designer: Amber Reed | Set Designer & Props: Cinnabar Inc. (Fabrication) | Writers: Carolyn Collins Petersen, Jeremy Bloom, Sophie Katz, Aaron Pope, and Michael Rigsby | Client: California Academy of Sciences

Description: The project consists of approximately 20,000 square feet of exhibits on the main floor of the new Renzo Piano-designed California Academy of Sciences in San Francisco, California. The principal exhibits are two galleries found at the east and west ends of the main hall. The east exhibit gallery, Islands of Evolution, examines the Academy's various expeditions and research in the Galapagos and Madagascar with a focus on evolution. The west gallery, Altered State: Climate Change in California, sets climate change in context: globally, in the state of California and locally. The exhibit looks at rising and acidifying oceans, melting ice, hotter and drier environments, and, finally, extinction to illustrate what we stand to lose. Visitors can learn about efforts to help mitigate the effects of climate change and also make individual pledges to alter their own impact on the planet.

118 VP | Design Firm: Lorenc+Yoo Design, Roswell | Account Director: Marcus Merritt | Design Director: Jan Lorenc | Photographer: Deborah Wolfe | Print Producer: Henry Incorporated | Senior Designer: David Park | Client: Cousins Properties Inc. John McColl

Description: Lorenc+Yoo Design was brought in to design canopies for a 15-year-old building designed by Philip Johnson in downtown Atlanta. The building appeared to have a presence of a Cathedral with little or no identification as to who was inside. LYD was commissioned to design a people- scaled series of canopies that allow for building identification as well as that of its major anchors. LYD studied the scale, the color and the classical design tied to the powerful building architecture. Context was an important part of this design. One major central canopy 33" wide x 12" deep x 5" high, one restaurant canopy for Il Molino 17" wide x 8" deep x 4 high on the left side and one amenity directory sign 17" wide 4" deep x 9" high on the left. The 191 tower is a 55-story corporate office building in downtown Atlanta it is currently the regional headquarters for Deloitte.

119 VP | Design Firm: Lorenc+Yoo Design, Roswell | Account Director, Design Director: Jan Lorenc | Designer, Photographer: David Park | Print Producer: Identities Architectural Specialties 1060 Union Center Dr. | Senior Designer: Steve McCall | Client: Hines Interests LP, General Electric Asset Management

Description: Lorenc+Yoo Design was brought in to design a restaurant canopy for this building designed by Jon Pickard of Pickard/Chilton of New Haven CT in midtown Atlanta. LYD was commissioned to design a canopy structure that related to the clean vertical lines and the sinuous curve of the building top and anchored itself at the base of the building. The restaurant designed and installed its own canopy and the building owner rejected this design and installation and commissioned LYD to redesign the canopy paying homage to this very important Atlanta tower. LYD designed this canopy to visually join the building to have it be approved as part and parcel of the building and not a separate sign which would not be approved by the Midtown Alliance.This criteria resulted in a context-specific design which is an architectural accent to the building allowing it to gracefully engage the plaza located on Peachtree Street. Design of a single curved canopy which is made in three connected sections all reconnected to appear that it is part of the building. The right and left side have four columns attaching it to the ground plane and the TAP logo, which is the logo of the Brew House, was designed like a beer barrel that makes its way back to the building with a canopy underneath allowing the client to enter the space under cover. The right and left side are X' wide and Y' deep x Z' deep. These two joined canopies have louvers to block the heat of the noonday sun and have clear glass overhead to shhield the patrons from rain. They each have two uplights to wash the underside of the canopy and numerous downlights to wash the patrons dining below. The middle portion is a 6"diameter cylinder with an internally lit TAP logo on its face. The logo is also lit by an aura of light around the barrel as an accent. The 55-story tower is an icon tower in Midtown Atlanta giving a sinuous two hand embracing profile to the skyline. The treatment at the base of the building was important to keep the inherent value of the overall building intact and not let the retail tenants canopy take over the importance of the ground plane. The right and left side are 12' high, the center of the canopy curves up to 18' high and the overall width is 68', depth is 9' and a 3' extension at the cylinder back to connect to the building sun screens to make it a part of the building.

120 Syracuse University/S. I. Newhouse School of Public Communications Donor Wall | Design Firm: Poulin + Morris Inc., New York | Creative Director: Richard Poulin | Designers: Richard Poulin, Brian Brindisi, Alpkan Kirayoglu | Client: Polshek Partnership Architects

Description: Poulin + Morris was commissioned by Polshek Partnership Architects to develop an overall environmental graphics and donor recognition sign program to link the various areas of Newhouse III, the latest building in the S. I. Newhouse School of Public Communications complex. The visual solutions implemented rely upon the use of visual metaphor and technology to communicate the foundation and future mission of this premiere school of journalism. A unique donor recognition wall located in the building entrance lobby acknowledges the digital evolution of public communications by using a kinetic medium to communicate donor names and personal messages to passers-by. Over one hundred, staggered, horizontal LED digital panels display this information in a fluid, synchronized pace simulating multiple news zippers communicating simultaneously as if "real time" information were being displayed. Poulin + Morris' inspiration was to use LED technology in a non-conventional setting to symbolize the tenet "the medium is the message". Poulin + Morris' dynamic visual solutions function as meaningful and memorable symbols for the School. The solutions needed to be rich and engaging; not only to inspire, but to connect with the spirit, energy, diversity, professionalism, and creativity of past, present, and future generations.

121 Newseum/Freedom Forum Food Section Murals | Design Firm: Poulin + Morris Inc., New York | Creative Director: Douglas Morris | Designers: Douglas Morris, Brian Brindisi, AJ Mapes | Client: Polshek Partnership Architects

Description: Wall murals located in "The Food Section", the museum's international café, depict bold, colorful, large-scale images of food such as fruits, vegetables, grains, and the like. As the visitor approaches an image, a calculated optical illusion reveals typography, consisting of thousands of small-scale words containing ingredients and fares from around the world.

122 zebra crossing | Design Firm: design center ltd., Ljubljana | Art Directors, Authors, Creative Directors, Design Directors, Designers, Photographer: Eduard Cehovin, Tanja Devetak | Client: The City of Ljubljana

Description: The ZEBRA project incorporates the creative practice of visual communication into existing road markings. The latter are produced according to the Rules on Road Markings. According to the Rules, pedestrian crossings, or so-called zebra crossings, should be at least 4 metres wide. They can be marked by equal white lines that are 50 centimeters wide and with 50 centimetres wide spaces in between, or are demarcated along the width at the ends by white line markings, which are 10 centimetres wide, with the width of the field measuring 380 centimetres. The ZEBRA project redefines the visual image of road markings, where their functionality and choice of color remain the same. The public users accept the ZEBRA project as classical pedestrian crossing only that it gives more human faces of the road markings. In this sense, it gives design a public character that expresses good codes of practice with its innovative expression.

123 Tree by Tree, from Sea to Mountains | Design Firm: Rebeca Méndez Design, Los Angeles | Account Director, Art Director, Artist, Creative Director, Designer, Design Director, Photographer, Typographer: Rebeca Méndez | Associate Creative Directors: Adam Eeuwens, Rebeca Méndez | Client: LA County Arts Commission

Description: Rebeca Méndez was commissioned by the Los Angeles County Arts Commission to create an permanent art installation for the Los Angeles County Registrar-Recorder/County Clerk warehouse in Santa Fe Springs, Los Angeles County, CA. The RR/CC Warehouse stores birth, marriage, death and property records, plus it administers the elections. As such, the organization enables democracy and indirectly civilization by providing an infrastructure that legitimizes every citizen's identity and resulting rights. There is a registration of your life, and your significance is recorded. I chose the tree as a metaphor for its connotation of dignity and growth. In addition, in the 21st century, Los Angeles is home to a rich urban forest where over 1,000 different species, varieties and cultivators coexist, and, like its people, LA's tree population is known as among the most diverse in the world.

The concept of this artwork is inspired by the central imagery of the Los Angeles County seal, where a dignified Native American woman with a plate of nourishment in her hands stands on the shore of the Pacific Ocean with the San Gabriel Mountains in the background. In the artwork, the viewer's point of view moves in a 180° skyward pan from the Pacific Ocean to the San Gabriel Mountains. In its trajectory, the viewer encounters branches, tree trunks, the full canopy of diverse tree tops, and open sky, all from human scale. In a sense, the viewer is the woman in the seal. She is the trees, she is Mother Earth. The extreme length and the diagonal placement of the artwork within the architecture, adds a cross-rhythmic play to the space, activating and dynamically connecting the three of the large architectural volumes. The artwork is a single (no seams) large format and high-resolution photographic inkjet print, measuring 132 by 15 feet, printed on BIOflex, a fire-retardant and biodegradable vinyl, printed by local supergraphics studio Olson Visual. The structure is held by steel tubes assembled on location and inserted in a top and bottom pocket. The hanging mechanism is from Arakawa Systems.

Exhibits

124, 125 Robots Exhibit | Design Firm: Pentagram, San Francisco | Creative Director: Kit Hinrichs | Designers: Kit Hinrichs, Maurice Woods | Client: EMP/SFM Seattle

Description: Celebrating our fascination with humankind's technological version of itself, this exhibition designed by Kit Hinrichs for the Experience Music Project and Science Fiction Museum in Seattle, Washington draws from a one-of-a-kind assemblage of toy robots from the collection of noted designer Tom Geismar, founder and principal of Chermayeff & Geismar. Inspired by antique tin and wooden toys, samurai warriors and mid-20th century Japanese film characters, these intricately detailed miniatures are displayed almost like jewelry in a large, bottom-lit case and surrounded by ten foot tall photo murals of the same robots to create a unique juxtaposition of imagery. The descriptive signage is "held" by giant 2-dimensional robots as you walk around the exhibition.

126-128 Long May She Wave Exhibit | Design Firm: Pentagram, San Francisco | Creative Director: Kit Hinrichs | Designers: Kit Hinrichs, Gloria Hiek | Client: Nevada Museum of Art

Description: In his search to understand what is iconic, Hinrichs has been fascinated with the many graphic interpretations of the American flag and how the elements in its design can be parsed into individual colors and patterns and yet be recognizable to millions around the world. The Stars and Stripes is a national brand, a logo and a symbol that is filled with emotion and levels of meaning that change with the political and cultural climate of the times. This 8,500 square foot exhibition is on display at the Nevada Museum of Art in Reno and includes Civil War-era flags, handmade quilts, hundreds of toy flag bearer soldiers, weather vanes, jewelry, Native American weavings, political campaign memorabilia, clothing and protest banners, packaging labels and fine arts photographs.

129-131 Alphabetilately A-Z Exhibit | Design Firm: Michael Osborne Studio, San Francisco | Creative Director: Michael Osborne | Designer: Cody Dingle | Writer: Alyson Kuhn | Client: Smithsonian National Postal Museum

132 X Exhibition Space | Design Firm: Sense Team, Shenzhen | Account Director: Yvonne Zhong | Art Director, Creative Director: Hei Yiyang | Designers: Hei Yiyang, Liu Zhao, Zhao Meng, Zhan Ting, Huang Moqiu, Li Jia | Photographer: Zhang Qing | Client: SGDA & LOOOK

Description: As one of the exhibitions that can display the talents of 11 young designers from 5 countries around the world, the lights symbolize the spurt of creation ideas. The venue also separates these exhibitors from various space, which has greatly lent colour to the secret atmosphere of the opening ceremony.

133 Fuego Tradeshow Booth | Design Firm: Pentagram, San Francisco | Creative Director: Kit Hinrichs | Designer: Eric Schmidt | Client: Fuego

134 AGRIMED 2008 | Design Firm: Kibirt & Calce, Bari | Client: Regione Puglia - Assessorato Risorse Agroalimentari

Description: Study of an exhibition concept for the Apulia Region, Councillorship of Agrifood Resources. The Department of Agrifood Resources of the Apulia Region has participated in the 72nd edition of the Fiera del Levante, the most important Southern Italian traditional showcase, with an exhibition area of 3000 sq m. It was called "Agrimed" and is traditionally dedicated to the promotion of the territory's excellences, involving institutions, research institutes, the world of training, producers, category and consumer associations, with one million visitors. The goal was to offer the Apulia brand in a distinctive format that, for the quality of the products and the values of the productive processes, would position the region in a target of enogastronomic excellence.

The project – In a historical phase where the processes of purchasing and consumption of agrifood products seems to depend more on the current global tendencies and on the strength of multinational corporations in orientating, through marketing and communication, the fruition of goods, it has been decided to give back "Taste" as a value. Taste, like litmus of quality, is a subjective parameter that determines the "conscious" consumer's choice but is also a distinctive characteristic of the "good" product, the territory of its origin and reclaims the identity, also agrifood. Taste, if faithful, promotes itself and, even if it has an unquestionable objective, valences in the subjectivity of comparison. A Taste responding to these characteristics cannot but be greater. The slogan chosen for the Agrimed pavilion, which has become the leader of all the developed initiatives, is, "Taste is greater". The exhibition area was separated into sections with a communicative graphic format. The impact of an open space, which differentiates environments with their own thematic characterization, gradually creates a discovery path. The choice of a sober but elegant style gave life to a personalized concept that all the spaces benefited from. The "macro" images, featuring shapes and "tasty" colors, were used to express the greatness of the taste and the products of Apulia. The project has been proposed as a sensorial path, thanks to the great visual impact of the external surface of grapes, cherries, peppers, oranges, etc, which stimulated sight, touch and palate. In this exhibition area, the visitor was invited to enter the taste and become a conscious protagonist.

The institutional area – The institutional area gave hospitality to "Gusto di Puglia" (Taste of Apulia), a restaurant, ran by Slow Food, used for wine and local products tasting, as a laboratory of taste, a convention hall, Apulia's olive oil and wine cellars, an exhibition space for local products and an area for the meeting of operators.

The thematic area – The public benefited from the four thematic areas that, through images, videos and texts, displayed the attention and the sensitive commitment of the Councillorship of Agrifood Resources of the Apulia Region towards solidarity, food education, the Mediterranean gastronomical culture, and art. With this area were four separate spaces, Space 1: Solidarity Taste, Space 2: Art Taste, Space 3: World Taste and Space 4: Knowledge Taste.

135 10yearsOris50 (10godinaOris50) | Design Firm: Studio Rasic, Zagreb | Art Director: Ante Rasic | Designers: Lovorka Decker, Marko Rasic, Vedrana Vrabec | Photographer: Damir Fabijanic | Client: Arhitekst

Description: The objective of this exhibition was to present 50 published numbers of a prominent architectural magazine in Croatia—Oris, at the event celebrating its 10 years of existence. The event-exhibition took place in a circular "Croatian Academy of Sciences and Arts" building in Zagreb (Croatia) and it lasted one week.

In the center of the building, 50 magazine covers, enlarged and printed in a citylight technique were hung from the ceiling at different lengths, and illuminated by the natural light from the ceiling. 50 of the actual published numbers of Oris were exhibited on the circular wall placed in plexiglass panels. Also, 7 different LCD screens with Nintendo controllers were part of the exhibition, allowing the visitor to view an animated presentation of the magazine and all other work associated with the magazine such as published books, symposiums and events organized by Oris.

Illustration

136 induction | Design Firm: Peter Kraemer, Duesseldorf | Art Director: Christy Gray | Illustrator: Peter Kraemer | Client: Subzero/Wolf

Description: Illustration of a halved frying pan on an induction hob with an egg sunny side up. The egg is fried on the pan side and raw on the induction field to illustrate how induction cooking works.

137 The Sexual Male Part V | Design Firm: Mirko Ilic Corp, New York | Art Director: Rob Wilson | Illustrator: Mirko Ilic | Client: Playboy

138 Thunderstruck Cartooning Portfolio Magazine | Design Firm: Visual Arts Press, Ltd., New York | Art Director: Michael J. Walsh | Creative Director: Anthony P. Rhodes | Designer: Brian E. Smith | Client: School of Visual Arts

Description: Cartooning Portfolio Magazine is an anthology of work from

graduates of the class of 2007 in the BFA Illustration and Cartooning Department at SVA.

139 Personality | Design Firm: Jones Worldwide, Chicago | Artist: Jack Unruh | Creative Directors: Scott Maney, Dan Madole | Executive Creative Director: Scott Maney | Designer: Gus Granger | Client: Headwaters MB

Description: These illustrations were a series of drawings depicting the managing partners of a Denver based investment bank. Each illustration captured the partner's personality as well as reflected a differentiating point about the firm itself. The illustrations were used on their website and marketing materials to lure new clients. No pun intended.

140 The Post-Catastrophe Economy | Design Firm: Mirko Ilic Corp | Art Director: Joseph Perez | Illustrator: Mirko Ilic | Client: Penguin USA

141 Cosi Fan Tutte | Design Firm: René Milot Illustration Inc. | Art Director, Illustrator: René Milot | Creative Strategist: Christopher Milligan | Client: Cincinnati Opera

Description: Cosi Fan Tutte – Cincinnati Opera poster (Summer 2007): Mozart's opera dealing with the frailty of love that is easily blinded by seduction. Digital illustration.

142 Bette Davis | Design Firm: PhotoAssist, Inc., Bethesda | Art Director, Designer, Typographer: Richard Sheaff | Artist: Michael J. Deas | Client: United States Postal Service

143 Edgar Allan Poe | Design Firm: PhotoAssist, Inc., Bethesda | Art Director, Designer, Typographer: Carl T. Herrman | Artist: Michael J. Deas | Client: United States Postal Service

Interactive

144, 145 PLATINUM Kotonohagusa - Japanese lifestyle with traditional 24 seasons | Design Firm: Business Architects Inc., Tokyo | Art Director: Yukihiko Kuroda | Creative Director: Yu Morita | Designers: Hirohito Fukutomi, Tomokazu Kitamura, Yasutaka Kageyama, Shinya Kobayashi, Masaomi Kurihara | Programmer: Koji Kasugai | Project Managers: Masahiro Wada, Fumito Sato, Akane Sakita | Writer: Hiroyo Horiguchi | Client: iTV Co., Ltd.

Description: This site is a special content site within the tourism portal for Mie-Prefecture, "Travel Iseshima, Yoitokose." Based on the traditional calendar where the year is divided into 24 segments of 15 days each, it features the rich cultural tradition of the Japanese life. By showing the culture of Iseshima, its seasons, nature and food it shows that all seasons and cultural traditions were tied into the now forgotten old way of living. The goal of this content is to create a sense of nostalgia and allow the users to sit back and remember a time when seasons, nature and a slower pace of life once was.

146, 147 Company Website | Design Firm: Visual Voice, Oak Park | Creative Director: Kayo Takasugi | Designers: Mark Stammers, Kayo Takasugi | Photographer: Hemmant Jha | Client: think/thing

148 www.scottiesboutique.co.nz | Design Firm: Alt Group, Auckland | Creative Director: Dean Poole | Design Director: Toby Curnow | Designer: Nadia Aftimos | Photographer: Deborah Smith | Client: Scottie Boutique

Description: Marilyn Sainty's fashion intersects on the axis where elegance and outrageousness meet. The concept of the site was built around the idea of a gallery wall, a number of small works that could be unpacked to reveal a series of different experiences, still images, sound, animations and catwalk movies. The concept reflects the nature of the business, a highbrow fashion boutique, representing some of the most influential brands in global fashion.

149 www.dillerscofidio.com | Design Firm: Pentagram, New York | Creative Director: Lisa Strausfeld | Designers: Lisa Strausfeld, Takaaki Okada, Christian Marc Schmidt, Christian Croft, Christian Swinehart | Web Developers: Christian Croft, Christian Swinehart | Client: Diller Scofidio + Renfro

Description: Pentagram has designed the new website for Diller Scofidio + Renfro, the New York-based interdisciplinary studio that develops built and conceptual works encompassing architecture, urban design, site-specific installations and the visual and performing arts. DSR's recent projects include the design of the Institute of Contemporary Art in Boston, the current redevelopment of the Lincoln Center and the refurbishment of the High Line in New York. Lisa Strausfeld and her team worked closely with DSR to create a site that reflects the firm's unique, theory-driven approach. The visual style of the site was inspired by the firm's rendering technique in which projects are depicted as a montage of flat imagery within three-dimensional space. The site, also rendered in three dimensions, allows for pivotal navigation through a photo view or a text-based index view. Each project is allocated a position in a landscape-like arrangement that shifts on axis from a 3-D view (for the photo view) to a more two-dimensional reader or bird's eye view (for index view). Within each view, projects can be sorted chronologically or alphabetically, as well as be filtered by category. In the photo view, images of the sorted projects flip up or recede depending upon the criteria selected; in the index view, the chosen projects are highlighted in bold. In either view, examining projects in depth takes one through to the other side of words or images.

The site is built in Flash and uses Papervision3D, an open source 3D engine for Flash. Strausfeld also developed a content management system so DSR can continually update the site.

150 Schmitt Photography Website | Design Firm: Sibley/Peteet Design, Austin | Art Director, Web Developer: David Guillory | Photographer: Tyler Schmitt | Client: Schmitt Photography

Description: Portfolio and informational website for Schmitt Photography.

151 Capital In Sight | Design Firm: The Halo Group, New York | Art Director: Wongi Ryu | Creative Director: Tim Woods | Client: Guy Carpenter

Description: Much like archery, reinsurance is incredibly complex requiring expertise and precision to execute. The smallest misstep could lead to millions of dollars lost. As a leading reinsurance broker, Guy Carpenter (GC) provides industry leading intellectual capital and innovative tools that give clients the confidence that their reinsurance solution will hit the target. Capital In Sight showcases Guy Carpenter's expertise in a new and creative way, injecting some fun and humor into a category with little history of marketing innovation, while also playing into the competitive nature of its clients and prospects. Featuring origami money from the current award-winning advertising campaign, game players must navigate disastrous factors to hit their targets. Using GC's tools and advice helps players get a more clear shot or understand how their arrows will fly. The game was launched at an annual Guy Carpenter event for clients and prospective clients, during which they competed for bragging rights and their name atop of the leader board. After its initial launch, the game was then used as a marketing tool for the sales team and is a main attraction on GC's new interactive marketing website.

Invitation

152 Holiday Card | Design Firm: JB Design, Norwalk | Account Director, Creative Director, Writer: J Berry | Client: JB Design

Description: 2008 Holiday Card.

153 A Night to Remember: BAFTA Themed Birthday (invite) | Design Firm: Turner Duckworth, San Francisco | Creative Directors: David Turner, Bruce Duckworth | Designer: Gavin Hurrell | Editor: Reuben James | Client: John Buckland

Description: When asked to create an invite for a BAFTA themed 50th birthday party, Turner Duckworth looked directly to classic films for inspiration. As you open the invite you realize each page uses a famous movie catchphrase, with instructions such as 'John Buckland requests the pleasure of your company…' turning into 'Here's Johnny!'. The formal white on black print, as well as a golden envelope, created a stylish invitation no one could turn down.

Letterheads

154 Alward Construction Branding | Design Firm: Craig-Teerlink Design, San Francisco | Creative Director, Designer: Jean Craig-Teerlink | Photographers: Dale Higgins, Frank Domin | Print Producers: Nora Chan, Golden Dragon Printing | Client: Alward Construction

Description: Alward Construction is a 50-person residential and commercial green building company, known for its sophisticated problem solving and integrity, practicing in the California Bay Area. All company communications, work sites, and vehicles were branded.

155 John P. McNulty Prize | Design Firm: Poulin + Morris Inc., New York | Creative Director: Richard Poulin | Designers: Richard Poulin, AJ Mapes | Photographer: Bill Hatcher/National Geographic Stock | Client: John P. and Anne Welsh McNulty Foundation

Description: The John P. McNulty Prize Letterhead was developed in coordination with an identity and branding program for the prize, as well as the John P. and Anne Welsh McNulty Foundation. The logotype and letterhead were designed to reflect the unique energetic character of John P. McNulty. The Prize was created in connection with the Aspen Institute, to celebrate the spirit and memory of John P. McNulty by supporting extraordinary young leaders making creative, effective, and long lasting contributions to their communities.

156 Corporate Collaterals | Design Firm: Coal Creative Consultants Pte Ltd, Singapore | Account Director: Goh Yong Yau | Art Director: Tan Eng Teck | Creative Director: June Thein | Client: Coal Creative Consultants Pte Ltd

157 Ambigram advertising agency Identity | Design Firm: Pentagram Design Ltd., Berlin | Art Director, Designer: Justus Oehler | Client: Ambigram

Description: Justus Oehler and his team designed the new identity and graphics program for Ambigram, an advertising agency start-up in Thessaloniki, Greece. The company chose as its name the word ambigram, which denotes a word or graphic that can be read when inverted, back to front and front to back, like OTTO (also a palindrome), or when rotated or flipped upside down, like the date 1961. As the name Ambigram did not present an easily read solution, Oehler decided to create a "meandering" logo that at first looks like a graphic device but then reveals its meaning. The identity appears in a simple gray or silver-on-white, but when applied to stationery, press kits and other printed materials, visual impact is created by placing the logo on a contrasting background that gradates from one CMYK color to another: cyan to magenta, cyan to yellow and magenta to yellow.

Logos

158 Dallas Pottery Invitational | Design Firm: Peterson Ray & Company, Dallas | Account Director, Creative Director, Designer: Scott Ray | Art Directors: Scott Ray, Dorit Suffness | Illustrators: Scott Ray, Nhan Pham | Client: Dallas Pottery Invitational

Description: An Annual Pottery Exhibit featuring artists from around the world.

159 PLATINUM Murray Piano Services | Design Firm: MacLaren McCann Calgary | Art Director, Creative Director, Designer: Mike Meadus | Client: Murray Piano Services

160 Logo | Design Firm: TompertDesign, Palo Alto | Creative Director: Claudia Huber Tompert | Designer: Anneka Cerny | Illustrator: Raygun Studio | Client: OsteoCorp

Description: OsteoCorp develops novel drugs that reverse the effects of osteoporosis by stimulating regrowth of new bone tissue.

161 (1st) Airlite Plastics Logo | Design Firm: Webster Design Associates, Omaha | Account Director: Lisa Hug | Art Director: Nate Perry | Creative Director: Dave Webster | Client: Airlite Plastics Co.

Description: Airlite Plastics Co. is an industry leader in plastic injection molding and printing, known for its innovative printing processes, package designs and product development. Airlite's previous logo included a DC-3 plane, which has become a part of its heritage and is recognized by its customers, prospects and competitors. The DC-3 was the most innovative plane of its time and has become Airlite's symbol for their "spirit of innovation".

161 (2nd) Verbal-Visual Framework Logo | Design Firm: Karen Lukas-Hardy Design, Duluth | Designer: Karen Lukas-Hardy | Client: Verbal-Visual Framework

Description: Logo design for Verbal-Visual Framework (VVF) brand-design research methodology. The VVF method clarifies how verbal brand attribute meaning resonates visually with target customers through a structured framework of referential associations. The quantitative approach structures the associations using semiotic algorithms and predictive analytics. Results provide the strategic connection between brand intent and customer desire. The logo design solution conveys the fundamental elements of VVF methodology in a clear, concise and compelling manner.

161 (3rd) Denver Mountain Parks | Design Firm: Michael Schwab Studio, San Anselmo | Creative Director: Tina Bishop | Designer, Illustrator: Michael Schwab | Client: Denver Mountain Parks

Description: The Denver Mountain Parks, owned and maintained by the City and County of Denver, is a historic system which was launched in 1910. This logo was created to evoke the strong, romantic history of the Parks.

161 (4th) Drake Wellington Logo | Design Firm: AG Creative, Vancouver | Account Director: Dave Ancrum | Creative Director, Designer: Stewart Jung | Client: Drake Wellington

Description: An investment firm who deals mainly in the European market. The logo was a play on the company name where Drake historically refers to Draco, a dragon, which symbolized strength and prosperity in many cultures. The client was thrilled.

161 (5th) Torchôn Catering Identity | Design Firm: Sibley/Peteet Design, Austin | Art Director: Rex Peteet | Creative Strategist: Elisha Moore | Designer, Illustrator: Flint LaCour | Client: Tôrchon Catering

Description: Tôrchon is a new catering company founded by Austin chefs, Jeremy Moore and James Flowers. With backgrounds in traditional French and Italian cooking, their style might be best described as "new classics,"—incorporating fresh flavors into traditional techniques. Reflecting this approach, the name Torchôn was taken from the traditional French method of preparing foie gras. Torchôn's focus is on in-home dinner parties, bringing a 4-star, private dining experience to the home. The identity's unique color palette and custom-made typeface are reminiscent of old-world sensibilities and yet, the overall appeal remains as warm, inviting and eclectic as the food for which Torchôn's chefs are known.

162 (1st) The National Museum of Nuclear Science & History Logo | Design Firm: 3 Advertising, Albuquerque | Account Director: Chris Moore | Creative Director: Sam Maclay | Design Director: Tim McGrath | Client: The National Museum of Nuclear Science & History

Description: A place where visitors are invited to think about and share their views of nuclear science and its role in the world, from war and peacekeeping to technology and medicine.

162 (2nd) Mending Homes | Design Firm: MacLaren McCann Calgary | Art Director, Creative Director, Designer, Illustrator: Mike Meadus | Client: Mending Homes

Description: Logo for residential repair company.

162 (3rd) Green is Beautiful Logo | Design Firm: Young & Laramore, Indianapolis | Account Director: Ann Beriault, Kurt Ashburn | Art Director, Associate Creative Director: Trevor Williams | Creative Director: Carolyn Hadlock | Designer: Elijah Schroeder | Illustrator: Mira Nameth | Writer: Scott King | Client: Brizo Faucet

162 (4th) One Eleven Logo | Design Firm: Visualink Creative, Franklin | Art Director, Designer: Grant Kennedy | Client: Event Logistics, Inc.

162 (5th) Tolga Os Sparebank | Design Firm: Strømme Throndsen Design | Creative Director: Morten Throndsen | Designers: Eia Grødal, Linda Gundersen | Typographers: Morten Throndsen, Richard Dawson | Client: Tolga Os Sparebank

Description: Tolga Os Sparebank is a local Norwegian Savings Bank. The new identity should convey the bank as the local hero; a solid, highly trustworthy bank with a positive and friendly service minded approach. The logo combines a classic typography with a square shape in red that is easy to recognize, communicating the local bank as the absolute hero in the local society.

163 Ta Ta Tee-shirt Logo | Design Firm: Brogan & Partners, Birmingham | Account Director: Ellyn Davidson | Art Director, Artist, Associate Creative Director, Designer, Illustrator: David Ryan | Author: Melissa Weber | Creative Director: Laurie Hix | Client: Ellyn Davidson

Description: This logo was used on a tee-shirt to attract attention of team members of the Ta Ta breast cancer 3-Day walk team.

164 M | Design Firm: Ron Taft Design, Los Angeles | Art Director, Chief Creative Officer, Designer: Ron Taft | Client: M-Fitzsimons

Description: M-Fitzsimons is a LEED architect who specializes in sustainable (Green) interior design.

165 (1st) Holland America Canaletto Logo | Design Firm: Hornall Anderson, Seattle | Design Directors: Lisa Cerveny, Julie Lock | Designers: Mary Hermes, Lauren DiRusso, Vu Nguyen | Illustrator: Georgia Deaver | Client: Holland America

165 (2nd) Brownstone Book Company Logo | Design Firm: TAXI CANADA INC, Canada | Account Director: Gord Ellis | Art Director: Kelsey Horne | Creative Director: Trent Burton | Illustrators: Kelsey Horne, Brad Connell | Print Producer: Marsha Walters | Client: Brownstone Book Company

Description: We set out to create a logo for Brownstone that would create a strong visual connection to books without having to use the word 'bookstore' itself. The logo contains a balance between the Brownstone name and the their product offering in a single glance.

165 (3rd) Islamorada | Design Firm: Colle + McVoy, Minneapolis | Client: Field and Stream

165 (4th) Holland America Slice Logo | Design Firm: Hornall Anderson, Seattle | Design Directors: Lisa Cerveny, Julie Lock | Designers: Lauren DiRusso, Vu Nguyen, Kathleen Kennelly Ullman | Client: Holland America

Credits&Comments

165 (5th) Presh Jewelry Logo | Design Firm: UNIT design collective, San Francisco | Creative Directors: Ann Jordan, Shardul Kiri | Designer: Ann Jordan | Client: Presh Jewelry

Description: For this jewelry design studio, we created a custom lettering style that highlights the designer's stylistic use of small stones and metallic beading that gracefully fall from each piece of jewelry.

166 (1st) Coffee Bean & Tea Leaf Logo | Design Firm: Hornall Anderson, Seattle | Design Director: Andrew Wicklund | Designers: Peter Anderson, Jay Hilburn, Kathleen Kennelly Ullman, Jessica Lennard | Client: Coffee Bean & Tea Leaf

166 (2nd) Harrison Pipelines | Design Firm: MacLaren McCann Calgary, Calgary | Art Director, Creative Director, Designer, Illustrator: Mike Meadus | Client: Harrison Pipelines

Description: Logo for pipeline manufacturing company.

166 (3rd) Corporate ID | Design Firm: Melissa Collins | Graphic Design, Bendemeer | Art Director, Designer: Melissa Collins | Client: Clevelands Wagyu

Description: Logo design for cattle company featuring Wagyu Cattle.

166 (4th) Mission Bean Coffee Logo | Design Firm: Bailey Lauerman, Lincoln | Art Directors, Designers: Ron Sack, James Strange | Creative Director: Carter Weitz | Illustrator: James Strange | Client: Mission Bean Coffee

166 (5th) BSEACD Identity | Design Firm: Sibley/Peteet Design, Austin | Account Director: Sherri Matthews Advocacy Marketing | Art Director: Rex Peteet | Designer, Illustrator: Oscar Morris | Client: Barton Spring Edwards Aquifer Conservation District

Description: The BSEACD is committed to conserving, protecting, recharging, and preventing waste of groundwater and to preserving all aquifers within the District. Their logo needed to represent the organization's role as a guardian of one of our most important resources.

167 Ovation Logo | Design Firm: Saatchi Design Worldwide, Auckland | Creative Director: Blake Enting | Design Director: Derek Lockwood | Senior Designer: Andy Scarth | Client: Ovation Limited

Description: OVATION. The live-event industry is fast moving and highly competitive. PeopleTech, as US-based business, realized they needed a fresh face and a new position in the market. Saatchi Design developed a new brand platform consisting of a new company name, brand strategy, organizing idea, logo, graphic treatment and photographic style. The result is a brand identity that sits comfortably in the corporate arena but still plays in creative space. Ovation's organizing idea; "Mastering Moments of Magic", is symbolized by the logo's magic black box and unites the business strategy with its creative services. A powerful brand that promises clients the perfect delivery.

168 (1st) Tru-Way Logo Design | Design Firm: Jessica Campbell, Chicago | Creative Director, Designer: Jessica Campbell | Client: Tru-Way Metal Fabrication

Description: The Chicago-based metal fabrication company needed a new logo design to promote their business. After visiting the factory and seeing a plethora of greased machinery, button controls, and equipment warning signs, I was inspired by the work environment. The logo acts much like a symbol that could be seen amongst the others in the factory. Depending on the orientation of the logo (vertically seen), it lends itself to a visual representation of the main drill found at the plant. Looking closely, it also spells "TW", the initials of Tru-Way.

168 (2nd) Penny Hay Logo | Design Firm: Saatchi Design Worldwide, Auckland | Creative Director: Blake Enting | Designer: George Kivell | Client: Penny Hay Limited

Description: The Client – Penny Hay is an Interior Architect, Artist and Collector. Her works, ranging from luxury residential homes to retail spaces, are filled with her custom designed furniture, fixtures and hand selected objects. *The Brief* – Create an identity that captures the character of Penny Hay, the Artist and Collector, while retaining the authority of an architectural practice. *Design Solution* – The squirrel was selected as a metaphor of how Penny Hay designs, collecting objects and ideas, storing them for future use, Its curved form is reminiscent of ornamental furniture. Classical typography and a simple black and white color palette deliver a timeless marque, both as a formal logo and an artist stamp to use on custom designs.

168 (3rd) Library Logo | Design Firm: Siegel+Gale, New York | Chief Creative Officer: Howard Belk | Creative Director: Matthias Mencke | Design Directors: Marcus Bartlett, Lloyd Blander | Executive Creative Director: Sven Seger | Client: Ronald Reagan Library

168 (4th) Okooko Logo | Design Firm: Saatchi Design Worldwide, Auckland | Creative Director: Blake Enting | Designers: Blake Enting, Andy Scarth, George Kivell | Client: Design Mobel

Description: Client – Design Mobel is a New Zealand bed manufacturer, focused on the science of sleep. Their bedroom products and accessories are made from sustainably harvested native New Zealand timber and manufactured from other sustainable and natural materials. / *Objective* – Create a retail brand and strategy strongly linked to New Zealand, that expands the brand offering beyond beds, with a softer, more emotive feel to balance the sleep science. / *Solution* – Based on the brand idea 'replenishment for a better life', the offering expanded from beds to 'bedroom sanctuaries'. The name Okooko is a Maori word meaning 'to cradle in arms'. The New Zealand forest, nature's sanctuary, became a visual metaphor to represent this core idea, and reinforced the sustainable position the business proudly holds. The four O's in the logo design incorporate a cultural fern motif, symbolic of life and growth. When used together they make the Okooko tree ring symbol, and this has been used as a key graphic device throughout the identity.

168 (5th) Lokale Helter Logo | Design Firm: Strømme Throndsen Design | Creative Director: Morten Throndsen | Designer: Linda Gundersen | Typographer: Morten Throndsen, Linda Gundersen, Richard Dawson | Client: Natural

Description: Lokale helter (Local heroes) is a new brand for organic products, based mainly on local produce.

169 MME Logo | Design Firm: modulation design, Kendall Park | Art Director: Craig Maher | Designers: Craig Maher, Paul Gaschler | Client: Multi Media Exposure

170, 171 IGH | Design Firm: STUDIO INTERNATIONAL, Zagreb | Account Director, Art Director, Artist, Author, Creative Director, Design Director, Designer, Typographer: Boris Ljubicic | Editor: IGH | General Director: Jure Radic / IGH | Illustrator: Igor Ljubicic | Client: IGH-Civil Enginering Institute of Croatia

Description: This Logo is for IGH (Civil Engineering Institute of Croatia). In 3D concept, IGH is the biggest engineering corporation in Central Europe. *Field of activity* – Research & development activities in the following scientific disciplines of civil engineering: geotechnics, construction materials, water engineering, load-bearing structures, construction management, transportation and structural mechanics / Research & development activities in the related scientific fields and disciplines / Testing and issuing test certificates for materials, structural assemblies, structures, support systems, soil, testing devices and production procedures / Improvement of the general, technical and autonomous regulations in the field of civil engineering and in other fields where knowledge of civil engineering is required; development and coordination relating to implementation of international regulations in the field of civil engineering / Improvement of development programs and construction technologies, preparation of studies on the environmental impact of structures, with a particular emphasis on the protection, preservation and improvement of the human environment / Research work in all fields of geo-sciences when related to civil engineering / Inspection of technical documents with respect to stability, safety, functionality, physical properties and cost-effectiveness / Consultancy services for the construction industry including: Expert supervision during construction works; Preparation of technical documents: designs, design concepts, bidding reports, studies; Economic, management-related and technological services; Physical planning - public services and utilities; Environment protection, improvement of land and technical equipment; Quality assurance for technical equipment of structures; Elaboration and implementation of quality assurance programs.

MusicCDs

172 New Zealand New Music CD Series | Design Firm: Alt Group | Creative Director: Dean Poole | Designers: Shabnam Shiwan, Dean Poole, Aaron Edwards, Tony Proffit | Photographer: Toaki Okano | Writer: Alt Group | Client: New Zealand Trade and Enterprise

Description: The objective was to promote New Zealand artists to decision makers in the international music industries, across a series of CD releases. Culture = Product = Culture. Because this is a DM project, the audience feels unencumbered, it is easy to simply throw the package away. The package is being sent to screen industry people that receive hundreds of CDs a week. It must be something they want to keep, but also fit into their world (it must fit on their shelves, for example). The package combines the ordinary—a cover, a booklet, a jewel case, with an aesthetic quality and unique elements that make it desirable.

The design solution implicitly states that the New Zealand music industry, and particularly the musicians / music companies represented on the CDs, are part of the global music business. They are, of the business, a musical culture packaged within an irreverent take on the first New Zealand music, the song of our native birds. Each CD cover features images that reference New Zealand's songbird, the Tui. Each package sent to industry decision makers also includes a specially-designed brooch that references elements in the CD cover composition—nest, egg, bird and a skull—and represent the life cycle. The DM package, CD and brooch, combines as a product that with a knowing and confident tone. The confidence is important—the apparent 'desecration' of the native birds is not the act of artists undervaluing their origins, rather it is the act of embracing the global nature of the art contained within, art that is the equal of that from other territories, and worthy of consideration.

173 Robbing The Devil | Design Firm: Chris van Diemen | Art Director: Jeroen van Erp | Photographer: Annaleen Louwes | Senior Designer, Typographer: Chris van Diemen | Client: The Inlaw Sisters

Description: 'Old time music from the Appalachian Mountains', packed in a square gatefold album sleeve housed in a semi-transparent slipcase. The honest and authentic feel in the design is accompanied with a straightforward cover photo made by Annaleen Louwes, which runs over the spine to the back. The inside liner notes by producer Dirk Powell are leading to the booklet and disc. The disc itself is presented in a black inner sleeve, which also shows the direct and clear (typo)graphic style which is bold and sensitive at the same time.

Outdoor

174 Critter Quest | Design Firm: BBDO West, San Francisco | Account Director: Kelly McGuirk | Art Directors: Jon Soto, Allison May | Associate Creative Director, Writer: Neil Levy | Executive Creative Directors: Jon Soto, Jim Lesser | Client: San Francisco Zoo

Description: A multi-media advertising campaign designed to get San Franciscans to reconnect with the San Francisco Zoo. Out-of-home boards were strategically placed around San Francisco in high foot traffic locations. Each board featured distinct parts of animals on white (butterfly wings, antlers, feathers) and small instructions that encouraged people to stand, have a friend take a picture with a camera phone and then upload it to a link (gallery@sfzoo.org). When people stood in front of the boards, the illusion that they had these animal parts coming from them was achieved. The submitted pictures then became the basis of an online photo gallery. The best photos were used in print advertising promoting the shelters around town as well as a walking tour featuring more animals at the zoo. The campaign spread virally over cell phones and became the content of numerous blogs, and personal websites. In addition, it provided the zoo with free branded content as anyone who took a photo (whether they submitted it to the site or not) ended up with a zoo logo right next to them in their photograph.

Packaging

175 Okanagan Spring Brewery Packaging System | **Design Firm: Subplot Design Inc., Vancouver | Art Director, Designer, Illustrator, Typographer: Matthew Clark | Creative Directors, Creative Strategists, Design Directors: Matthew Clark, Roy White | Photographer: Clinton Hussey | Writers: Matthew Clark, Jeff Lewis | Client: Okanagan Spring Brewery**

Description: In its first 20 years, Okanagan Spring had grown to become British Columbia's leading craft beer brand. Despite top marks for the liquid itself, the brand had low recall, poor differentiation, and had no unaided recall even among diehard fans. The objective was to reposition the brand and reinforce the all-natural, handcrafted positioning and emphasize their craft-brewing expertise.

176 Prairie Organic Vodka Bottle | **Design Firm: OLSON, Minneapolis | Associate Creative Director, Art Director, Designer: Jeff Berg | Creative Directors: Brien Grant, Brooke Dykema, Eric Luoma | Executive Creative Director: Tom Fugleberg | Writer: Eric Luoma | Client: Phillips Prairie Organic Vodka**

177 Dry Fly Logo | **Design Firm: HL2, Seattle | Chief Creative Officer: Ross West | Creative Director, Designer: Dave Estep | Print Producers: Heather Volk, Corey Simmons | Project Manager: Jen Shawver | Writer: Noah Tannen | Editor: Joe Ehrbar | Client: Dry Fly Distilling**

Description: In 2007, Dry Fly Distilling launched into the spirit market with three products including vodka, gin, and whiskey. It is the first micro distillery in Washington State since Prohibition and was created by two friends and avid fly fishermen. In order to be competitive in the current market, Dry Fly positioned itself as an ultra-premium product of small batch, hand-crafted spirits. Dry Fly strived to capture the spirit of the Pacific Northwest and the great outdoors with its iconic red fly that served as the bridge between the founder's passion for fly fishing and their new line of spirits.

178 Bowmore Single Scotch Whisky-Premium Range | **Design Firm: Breeze Creative Design Consultants, Glasgow | Creative Director: Craig Mackinlay | Client: Morrison Bowmore Distillers Limited**

Description: Bowmore Distillery—Islay's oldest distillery—recently released the Super Premium Rare Bowmore, this expression being a 40 Year Old Single Malt, which there are only 58 bottles available worldwide. This release is the start of a new "Premier" Range being offered by the distillery. Each stunning bottle has a solid copper closure and seal and is presented in a leather winged box with suede lining and drop-down walnut panel. Retailing at around £5,000, only the most aspirational of drinkers will get to enjoy this great whisky treasure!

179 Auchentoshan Single Scotch Whisky | **Design Firm: Breeze Creative Design Consultants, Glasgow | Creative Director: Craig Mackinlay | Client: Morrison Bowmore Distillers Limited**

Description: Breeze Creative has radically redesigned the Auchentoshan range which was in its previous guise for around 12 years. The new packaging plus the additional expressions have also been developed with a view to inspiring a new and slightly younger audience of emerging malt consumers whilst giving existing connoisseurs an extended taste experience.

The whisky itself is delicate on the palate with a fresh zesty profile and a lighter whisky experience altogether than one traditionally associates with malt. The packaging has been given a sleek, more contemporary and urban look, with its glass embellishment and embossed textured papers and boards. The pearlised packaging, unique bottle shape and use of tone will give the brand significantly increased presence in the international on and off trade.

180 Gentleman Jack | **Design Firm: Michael Osborne Design, San Francisco | Creative Director: Michael Osborne | Designer: Alice Koswara | Client: Jack Daniel's**

181 Black Butte Double X 22-oz Packaging | **Design Firm: tbd advertising, Bend | Account Director: Kevin Smyth | Art Director: Audelino Moreno | Chief Creative Officer: Paul Evers | Writer: Guy Ragnetti | Client: Deschutes Brewery**

Description: This was released to help celebrate the Deschutes Brewery's 20th Anniversary. The label for this special brew—a doubling-up on ingredients from their famous Black Butte Porter recipe—was printed with a silver metallic, a double-hit of black ink and a spot varnish to accentuate the swirl. To set it apart even more, the bottle tip was hand dipped in black wax.

182 Red Truck Wines | **Design Firm: Sage Brandworks, Lafayette | Artist: Dennis Ziemienski | Creative Director, Designer: Laura Cramer | Client: 585 Wine Partners**

Description: Our goal was to create a dynamic brand architecture for Red Truck Wines using iconic truck illustrations as the focal point of each label. The use of bold color clearly defines the specific varietals within each sub-line.

183 Cali 351 | **Design Firm: Vanderbyl Design, San Francisco | Art Director, Designer: Michael Vanderbyl | Client: Terrano Napa Valley**

184, 185 Farmgate Wines | **Design Firm: Alt Group, Auckland | Creative Director: Dean Poole | Designers: Dean Poole, Shabnam Shiwan, Tony Proffit | Photographer: Derek Henderson | Writer: Alt Group | Client: Terrano Napa Valley**

Description: The objective was to develop a brand that supported a new direct to consumer business model. Terrior is a French word that means the unique characteristics of a place—its geography, climatic conditions, soil, even its people. It translates loosely as "a sense of place." This concept of place—specifically Hawkes Bay New Zealand at the heart of Farmgate Wines. The concept of the label was supported by the name—Farmgate, a word that is embedded in New Zealand's agricultural heritage and that told a story of honesty and integrity. Farmgate as a concept is also important, as the wine is not distributed in supermarkets or traditional liquor outlets, but direct to consumers. As the wine is sold direct, the label needed to function differently—the focus was not on shelf presence but on developing stories and connections that could be passed onto others. Farmgate is built on the concept of community—it features portraits and stories of artisan food producers from the Hawkes Bay Region on each wine label. Each food producer is paired with a varietal wine style suited to be matched with their product, for example a barrel aged chardonnay with the cheese maker. The photographic style references August Sanders, "People of the 20th Century." Like Sanders' images, the portraits included on the wine labels are in a documentary style, capturing real people. The back label contains a short statement from the food producer as well as the winemaker's notes about the wine.

186 2008 Fashion Jewelry Packaging | **Design Firm: Monahan & Rhee, New York | Creative Directors, Designers: Jeff Monahan, Howard Rhee | Client: Vera Wang**

Description: Monahan & Rhee was hired by fashion house Vera Wang for a new packaging program for their 2008 Fashion Jewelry Collection. The fashion jewelry is created from a variety of unconventional materials including antique crystals, burnished metals, metalized fabrics, leathers, and linen.

The packaging derives its inspiration from Vera Wang's use of bows in her ready-to-wear collections. For the packaging program, Monahan & Rhee developed a new production technique to integrate the ribbon and bow directly into the boxes, enabling them to function simultaneously as brand identifier, adornment, and carrying handles. The color scheme is monochromatic, with subtle blind embossing presenting the brand's logomark.

187 Special Edition Vivienne Tam Mini 1000 | **Design Firm: Goodby, Silverstein & Partners, San Francisco | Account Director: Martha Jurzynski, Nancy Reyes | Account Manager: Julia Gilbert | Art Director: Tanner Shea | Assistant Account Manager: Katie Temple | Consumer Notebook Director of ID: Stacy Wolff | Consumer Notebook Marketing: Betsy Cluck | Creative Director, Partner: Steve Simpson | Designer: Vivienne Tam | Director, Global Marketing: Tracey Trachta | Global Initiatives: Kerry Chrapliwy | Global Marketing Director: Alan Wang | Group Creative Directors, Associate Partners: Rick Condos, Hunter Hindman | Senior Vice President, Global Marketing: Satjiv Chahil | Vice President, Global Marketing: David Roman | Writer: Michelle Hirschberg | Client: Hewlett-Packard**

Description: HP wanted to attract more women, so we decided to become the go-to technology brand for fashionistas by giving them another opportunity to express their style. We connected with world-class fashion designer, Vivienne Tam, to create a truly haute computer and to own the connection between fashion and technology. When Vivienne Tam showed her '09 Spring and Summer collection at Fashion Week, we saw the ultimate expression of digital couture. Vivienne's first model walked down the catwalk carrying the world's first digital clutch.

188 iLife and iWork Packaging | **Design Firm: Apple, Cupertino | Client: Apple**

189 Apple Notebooks | **Design Firm: Apple, Cupertino | Client: Apple**

190 Sidekick LX | **Design Firm: PhilippeBecker, San Francisco | Account Director: Scott Hagely | Creative Director: Phililippe Becker | Creative Strategist: Brody Hartman | Design Director: Jay Cabalquinto | Designers: Jay Cabalquinto, Mariko Harashima, Barkha Wadia | Photographer: Kevin Ng | Client: T-Mobile, USA**

Description: The packaging for the new T-Mobile Sidekick LX reveals a premium user experience to show off the sleeker, slimmer phone. The photograph of the phone with a white glow on a black background presents the product as the hero on the front of the sleeve while the inside box leverages a simple, clean design to highlight the phone's unique features.

191 PLATINUM Holli Mølle Special Edition | **Design Firm: Strømme Throndsen Design | Design Director: Morten Throndsen | Designers: Eia Grødal, Linda Gundersen | Client: Holli Mølle**

Description: Holli Mølle is an organic mill, using ancient and nutritious grain types in its production of flour. We have created a strong identity based on values such as tradition, organic production, environmentally friendly, and authenticity. This is the special edition that comes in a tin can that can be reused.

192 Estelle & Thild, Baby & Child | **Design Firm: Dolhem Design, Stockholm | Creative Director: Christophe Dolhem | Designer: Anna Lindelöw | Client: Estelle & Thild**

Description: Challenge – To differentiate the brand from both its large international competitors as well as smaller local brands whilst still communicating the natural origin of the products. / *Result* – A playful yet clean Scandinavian manner was applied on the packaging to appeal to aware parents with young children. The pattern of avocado leaves reappears throughout the Estelle & Thild profile, not only on the packages, as avocado oil is one of the most frequently used ingredients in the range. The pattern also symbolizes the natural origin of the products. The products are differentiated from each other by the mild pastel colours, often associated with children's products. Visually the product range stands out among its competitors.

193 826 Valencia | **Design Firm: Office, San Francisco | Creative Directors: Jason Schulte, Jill Robertson | Designers: Jason Schulte, Rob Alexander, Will Ecke, Gaelyn Mangrum, Jeff Bucholtz | Writers: Dave Eggers, Lisa Pemrick, Jon Adams, Dan Weiss, Jennifer Traig, Anna Ura, Rob Alexander, Ben Acker | Client: 826 Valencia**

Description: Office collaborated with 826 Valencia, a nonprofit tutoring center for kids, to reinvigorate San Francisco's only pirate supply store. Reflecting the store's wildly imaginative experience, the identity and nearly 50 new products represent 826's mission to support creative expression. All proceeds directly benefit the organization's free writing programs.

194 White Jasmine Sparkling Tea packaging | Design Firm: Elixir Design Inc., San Francisco | Creative Director: Jennifer Jerde | Designers: Aine Coughlan, Syd Buffman, Nathan Durrant | Photographer: David Liittschwager | Client: Golden Star Tea Co.

Description: The team at Golden Star Tea Co. developed the first-ever fermented sparkling floral tea. The organic infusion mimics the mouth-feel of champagne - without the alcohol. Through the packaging design, we helped blend the rich history of tea with ultra-premium positioning for this innovative sophisticated alternative to fine, still and sparkling wines.

195 Light Box | Design Firm: Kibrit & Calce, Bari | Designers: Maria Favia, Concetta Pastore | Client: Camera di Commercio di Bari

Description: Bari, December 2007.

Project – Study of a direct marketing action that promotes PDO extra virgin olive oil from the land of Bari for public reference. The client, the Chamber of Commerce, Industry, Handicraft and Agriculture of Bari, is committed to an intense act of support and enhancement of the excellent products of agriculture and agrifood of Bari, nationally and internationally.

The objective of the authority is also to overcome the fragmentation of the local productive fabrics and promote brand policies, in particular for products highly exposed to the competition, so a single label can collect more producers and can guarantee the volumes of sales capable of answering the demand of different markets. Terra di Bari extra virgin olive oil (Protected Designation of Origin) is the high band of an olive oil basin of over 80 thousand companies, 250 oil mills, more than 120 thousand hectares of cultivation, a total production per year of 1 million tons of product and connotes Bari's scenery and agriculture in an unmistakable way. The cultivars involved in this project are the unmistakable DNA of the oil of Bari, the Coratina and Ogliarola, and use a range of tastes and shades of color of the extraordinary organoleptic qualities. A thread of oil is like a beam of light: through direct marketing, which has been addressed to authoritative recipients (chefs, restaurant owners selected by authoritative guises, very qualified reception facilities, olive oil cellars), we wanted to point out the ability of Terrra di Bari PDO oil to "illuminate" plates and dishes and emphasize the healthy value of this cardinal product of the Mediterranean diet, which can be more than just a simple condiment, and whose luminosity, even in a bottle, remains faithful to the splendid light of the lands it comes from. / The package – Light Box is a special pack that contains two bottles of oil. Unique in its design and planning, Light Box was created by two Apulian craftsmen with precious materials that exalt the uniqueness and preciousness of the content. The sides are made of shiny black milled Plexiglas. The front part is one colored serigraphed sliding door that, when lifted, allows two leds to be turned on at a high intensity that lights up the two bottles from the top. The inside of Light Box contains a compact neutral colored polypropylene light fixture, a wooden shaped like the bottom of the two bottles and a hat also made of listel wood dignified by the essence of oak. For the occasion, the bottles contained in the inside have been personalized by a label with an unpublished image and contain the words "PDO extra virgin olive oil from the land of Bari" containing Ogliarola oil and Coratina oil and they are accompanied by a bilingual leaflet that illustrates the peculiarities of the product. Light Box is provided with a second package made of black coupled cardboard, personalized serigraphed by two hot stamped colors perfectly created on the dimensions of the box. The Light Box project has been registered in the majority of the foreign states at the W.I.P.O. (World Intellectual Property Organization) for a term of 5 years and it's renewable up to 25 years.

196, 197 PLUSX CUBE | Design Firm: MIYAGRAPHIX, Tokyo | Art Director, Designer: Manabu Miya | Creative Director: Kazuo Yana | Client: Lotte Co., Ltd. Products Planning Dept.

Description: Presentation of new package design in Japan.

198 (1st) Robert Harris - Occasions range | Design Firm: Dow Design, Auckland | Account Director: Carolynn Easton | Creative Director: Donna McCort | Designer: Dana Winter | Executive Director: Annie Dow | Photographer: Chris Sisarich | Client: Cerebos Gregg's Ltd

Description: Robert Harris is New Zealand's largest fresh coffee brand. Their diverse portfolio covers retail, cafés and food service. They were facing increasing competition from new entrants and international heavyweights. The challenge for the retail packaging sold in supermarkets was to unearth the essence that gave them a standout powerful consumer proposition. The idea was to bring to life the story of Robert Harris, the Kiwi coffee brand which started New Zealand's coffee culture. It has a passion for coffee and that intertwined with Kiwi attitude and heritage gave the company a unique position. The revamped brand packaging tells this story of Kiwi can-do spirit and passion, evoking relaxed moods & moments for the easy-going Occasions range.

198 (2nd) barista@home - ULTIMO | Design Firm: Dow Design, Auckland | Account Director: Carolynn Easton | Creative Director: Donna McCort | Designer: Dana Winter | Executive Director: Annie Dow | Client: Cerebos Gregg's Ltd

Description: Robert Harris is New Zealand's largest fresh coffee brand. With the challenge of increasing competition, the brief was to create a new brand voice for Robert Harris barista@home that was brave, edgy and relevant. It needed to appeal to the discerning coffee buyer and have shelf standout in the supermarkets. The solution was to express the new Robert Harris personality while keeping the Robert Harris name (a mainstream brand) low key. The new packs speak to the coffee connoisseur with a sense of individuality & urban attitude, but their bold, expressive style and simple straight-forwardness are pure Kiwi Robert Harris.

198 (3rd) Robert Harris - Selections range | Design Firm: Dow Design, Auckland | Account Director: Carolynn Easton | Creative Director: Donna McCort | Designer: Dana Winter | Executive Director: Annie Dow | Illustrator: Leonie Whyte | Client: Cerebos Gregg's Ltd

Description: Robert Harris is New Zealand's largest fresh coffee brand. Their diverse portfolio covers retail, cafés and food service. They were facing increasing competition from new entrants and international heavyweights. The challenge for the retail packaging sold in supermarkets was to unearth the essence that gave them a standout consumer proposition. The idea was to bring to life the story of Robert Harris, the Kiwi coffee brand which started New Zealand's coffee culture. The Selections range celebrates their passion for coffee as the original importer and roaster. That, intertwined with their Kiwi heritage highlighted in the illustrations, gives the packaging a unique position.

199 SosoFactory Salt | Design Firm: Eduardo del Fraile, Murcia | Creative Director, Designer: Eduardo del Fraile | Senior Designers: Andres Guerrero, Bruno Baeza | Client: Soso Factory

Description: A variety of salts of mass consumption, the containers of which can be distinguished by the initials of each salt flavour. These initials are inspired in the periodic table of elements.

Posters

200 Mirko Ilic Subway Poster | Design Firm: Visual Arts Press, Ltd., New York | Art Director: Michael J. Walsh | Artist, Designer: Mirko Ilic | Creative Director: Anthony P. Rhodes | Client: School of Visual Arts

Description: School of Visual Arts poster placed on New York City subway platforms intended for prospective students and the entire SVA community.

201 King Lear | Design Firm: WONGDOODY, Seattle | Associate Creative Director, Designer: Ross Hogin | Executive Creative Director: Tracy Wong | Print Producer: Stacy McCann | Project Manager: Eva Doak | Client: Rough Play Production

202 EyeSaw | Design Firm: Landor Associates, Sydney | Art Director, Creative Director, Creative Strategist, Writer: Jason Little | Designers: Jason Little, Ivana Martinovic, Sam Pemberton, Joao Peres | Executive Creative Director: Mike Staniford | Illustrator: Joao Peres | Typographer: Jason Little, Joao Peres | Client: AGDA / Sydney Design '08

Description: EyeSaw is a graphic design exhibition organized by the Australian Graphic Design Association (AGDA) and Sydney Design '08. It takes place in various outdoor locations throughout the city. Key objectives are to enable the public to engage with and discuss design; promote an understanding of what graphic design is to as many people as possible; broaden the promotion of graphic design to Australia. The brief was to create a smile in the mind whilst increasing the general publics awareness and recognition of graphic design. Our approach was to create a series of posters that play on some of the key traits associated with design: An eye for detail; an eye for colour; an eye for composition; an eye for beauty.

203 PENGUIN POSTER | Design Firm: Japan, Hiroshima | Art Director, Creative Director, Writer: Kazuto Nakamura | Designers: Kazuto Nakamura, Shuji Nagato | Client: Penguin Graphics

Description: It is a corporate poster of "the penguin graphics" that it made for the Year of the Ox of the Japanese sexagenary cycle. While by one of them employed Matsuba of the bonsai, I expressed it by the illustration of the penguin. I was associated in the Year of the Ox and chose the horn of the ox to "Jin" (the trunk which became a bleached bone) of the bonsai. I followed the sturdiness that improved toward the sky even if a trunk died. I expressed enthusiasm I believed one's power, and to advance without losing in the severe times said the world financial crisis once in 100 years.

204 iPod nano Launch Backwall Posters | Design Firm: Apple, Cupertino | Client: Apple

205 X ExhibitionB | Design Firm: Sense Team, Shenzhen | Account Director: Yvonne Zhong | Art Director, Creative Director: Hei Yiyang | Designers: Hei Yiyang, Liu Zhao | Photographer: Zhang Qing | Client: SGDA & LOOOK

Description: The series are photographed for X exhibition.

The light installations, which spell the names of different designers, represent their design ways in various fields. They have entered into the public places in Shenzhen such as the supermarket/overbridge/garden/park and so on. It is just fit for the exhibition theme—Graphic Design In China.

206 The Geography of Curiosity | Design Firm: Vanderbyl Design, San Francisco | Art Director, Illustrator: Michael Vanderbyl | Designers: Michael Vanderbyl, Ellen Gould | Client: Gravity Free

207 Northern Arkansas ADC Poster | Design Firm: Pentagram Design, Austin | Art Director: DJ Stout | Photographer: Randal Ford | Client: Northern Arkansas ADC

Description: Promotional poster for educational seminar.

208 Mammoth Unbound Posters | Design Firm: Hornall Anderson, Seattle | Creative Directors: Jack Anderson, David Bates | Designer: Javas Lehn | Illustrator: Julie Lock | Client: Mammoth

209 Dead on Arrival | Design Firm: L&C Design Studio | Design Director: Yuan-Yuan Liu | Client: Green Power Association

Description: The UN's Intergovernmental Panel on Climate Change (IPCC) report says the rise in global temperatures could be as high as 6.4°C by 2100. Up to 30 percent of animal and plant species will be vulnerable to extinction if global temperatures rise by 1.5-2.5 degrees Celsius (2.7 to 4.5 Fahrenheit), global warming will cause extinction of a million species. You might say: so what? Who cares if we increase temperatures a degree or two? By the time we even know about it, the invisible killer, too much consumption and corporations have already murdered us. That is what will happen if we don't put a stop to global warming. Insisting that it's not too late and that there is still plenty that humans can do to hold off the worst. Please reduce consumption, be green and save our lovely planet.

210 Fries | Design Firm: MacLaren McCann Calgary | Art Directors: Brad Connell, Kelsey Horne | Creative Director: Mike Meadus | Photographer: Jason Stang | Writer: Nicolle Pittman | Client: Dietitians of Canada

211 Hardly Strictly Bluegrass | Design Firm: Goodby, Silverstein & Partners, San Francisco | Art Director, Photographer: Claude Shade | Executive Creative Director: Jeffrey Goodby | Client: Hardly Strictly Bluegrass

212 James Hackett Lecture | Design Firm: Landor Associates, Sydney | Art Directors: Jason Little, Joao Peres, Sam Pemberton | Creative Director: Jason Little | Designer, Illustrator, Typographer: Joao Peres | Executive Creative Director: Mike Staniford | Client: James Hackett

Description: For a lecture series where professionals from different industries present their craft, a poster was created to promote each speaker. The posters had to capture the individual essence of each speaker, hint at their topic area and cut through the visual clutter of a typical office environment. This was achieved through typographic experiments that gave a witty nod to each speaker while complementing their trade. The key idea for James Hackett, a motion graphics and broadcast designer, was to use the well known test card visual language to signify the talk broadcasting soon.

213 YUNISANG | Design Firm: design818, Koyang | Art Director, Designer, Typographer: Do-Hyung Kim | Client: Yun Isang Peace Foundation

Promotions
214 Xero Wine Bottle | Design Firm: Alt Group, Auckland | Creative Director: Dean Poole | Designer: Clem Devine | Writer: Alt Group | Client: Xero

Description: Xero is an online accounting system designed for small businesses and their advisors. The brief was to develop a direct mail piece to act as a general promotional gift supporting the company's product and positioning. The solution was to design a bottle of wine with the bottom line in mind.

215 Art Serving Capitalism | Design Firm: Goodby, Silverstein & Partners, San Francisco | Client: Goodby, Silverstein & Partners

Description: We believe that great and highly effective advertising at its best is art. Or pretty much none of us would have gotten into advertising in the first place. Of course, the most important part of this thinking would be the last two words: serving capitalism. The art we make has to serve the needs of our clients. Or it's just art. Inspired by classic commercial art of the 1950s, these posters were designed to express this.

216 Sitting Pretty posters | Design Firm: Hoyne Design, St Kilda | Creative Director: Andrew Hoyne | Designers: Domenic Minieri, Felicity Davison | Photographer: Dean Tirkot | Client: Hoyne Design

217 Squires Holiday Card | Design Firm: Squires & Company, Dallas | Art Director: Laura Root | Designers: Laura Root, Jerome Marshall | Client: Squires & Company

Description: This piece was designed to be a holiday card for Squires & Company design firm.

218 Beckett Cambric Linen Paper Promotion | Design Firm: Michael Osborne Design, San Francisco | Creative Director: Michael Osborne | Designer: Alice Koswara | Writer: Alyson Kuhn | Client: Mohawk

219 Photography Portfolio Class of 2007 | Design Firm: Visual Arts Press, Ltd., New York | Art Director: Michael J. Walsh | Creative Director: Anthony P. Rhodes | Designer: Patrick Tobin | Client: School of Visual Arts

Description: A portfolio of work of the BFA Photography class of 2007. It is used to promote the BFA Photography department at SVA.

220, 221 METAL | Design Firm: Manarchy Films, Chicago | Art Director: Peter Van Vliet | Editor: Mary Beth Manarchy | Hair, Makeup: Cindy Adams | Photographer: Dennis Manarchy | Print Producer: Abbey Rose | Writer: Carla Barger | Client: Manarchy Films

Description: Hoodwinks. Prosthetics. 19th century smoke helmets. Art deco French beauty aids. Anti-baldness gadgets. Civil war mortician's reconstruction kits. Industrial safety equipment. Obsolete instruments of the early mental health industry. This is METAL; a series based on the collection of a man called simply, The Radio Guy. A certain cliché regarding pure design is:

form follows function. METAL is the opposite: form inspires perception. The Radio Guy, who at one time was an apprentice under the brilliant streamline designer, Raymond Loewy, recognized this fact. What may initially seem like a rather eclectic collection of contraptions is really very visually cohesive. One really only needs a couple electrodes and an outlet to administer electroshock therapy, but add a touch of "Metropolis", a few bands of sleek metal, and the whole thing jump-starts the imagination. Needless to say, this project brought me great satisfaction, especially since I was able to add a bit of my own alchemy. – *Dennis Manarchy*

222, 223 Apple Store Boylston Street Grand Opening | Design Firm: Apple, Cupertino | Client: Apple

ShoppingBags
224 Conference Bag | Design Firm: The Halo Group, New York | Creative Director: Joseph Reeves | Executive Creative Director: Tim Woods | Writer: Meg Moody | Client: St. George's University

Description: This bag was originally created as a promotional hand out for the National Association of Advisors for the Health Professions' (NAAHP) Annual conference. Since St. George's University is primarily a Medical and Veterinary Medical University, this campaign emphasized the increasingly common interconnections between animals and humans, which was the key insight to the campaign. The goal of this piece was to create a memorable, and interactive experience while simultaneously serving as an extension of the overall campaign.

225 The Big T Bag | Design Firm: ArthurSteenHorneAdamson, Cheltenham | Account Director: Mike Horne | Creative Director: Scott McGuffie | Designer: Leanne Thomas | Executive Creative Director: Marksteen Adamson | Hair: Richard Delingpole | Illustrator: Cathie Bleck | Project Manager: Kris Coppock | Client: Good Earth

226 (1st) Bendon Shopping Bags | Design Firm: Saatchi Design Worldwide, Auckland | Creative Director: Blake Enting | Design Director: Derek Lockwood | Illustrator: Jo Tronc (Watermark Limited) | Senior Designer: Kane McPherson | Client: Bendon

Description: Client – Bendon Lingerie is an international lingerie retailer that manufactures and sells a variety of lingerie labels, from Elle Macpherson and Bendon, to Hey Sister and Fayreform.
Objective – To create a retail carry-bag solution that further enhances the brand position—The Art of Curve Couture—and reflects the newly developed logo.
Solution – To develop an illustration style that celebrates two things:
1. The craft of lingerie – reflected in the intricate line work;
2. The feminine form – shaped with typography in a natural, written style.
This was applied to the two bag designs. They have had a powerful impact on the high street and connect directly with the consumer from both sexes.

226 (2nd) Trelise Cooper Kids Shopping Bags | Design Firm: Saatchi Design Worldwide, Auckland | Creative Director: Blake Enting | Design Director: Derek Lockwood | Illustrator: Anton Petrov (Watermark Limited) | Senior Designer: Kane McPherson | Client: Trelise Cooper

Description: The store creates a natural fantasy-filled environment where little girls aged 2-9 can explore feminine fashion. Merchandise complements this theme with imagery of spring meadow meets rainforest littered with hidden fairies and butterflies.

Signage
227 Grocery overhead | Design Firm: KNOCK inc., Minneapolis | Account Director: Jodi Grundyson | Associate Creative Director: KNOCK inc. | Creative Director: Todd Paulson | Design Director: KNOCK inc. | Designer: Rachel Nybeck | General Director: KNOCK inc. | Managing Director: Michael Doyle (Target) | Photographer: Erwan Frotin | Project Managers: Steve Prentice, Carey Kasbohm (Target) | Senior Designer: Ryan Floss | Client: Target

Description: Target was about to freshen up their offering by adding a produce section in many stores. KNOCK was picked to harvest a unique and inviting look for the new cornucopia. Simple, playful messaging, and a new photography style combined to capture the essence of fresh while remaining whimsical and fun. Meanwhile, a drop-down light drum overhead defined this new space and became a shining beacon of freshness for all guests.

Stamps
228 Charles + Ray Eames | Design Firm: PhotoAssist, Inc., Bethesda | Art Director, Designer, Typographer: Derry Noyes | Client: United States Postal Service

229 (1st) Mount Rushmore Priority Mail | Design Firm: PhotoAssist, Inc., Bethesda | Art Director, Designer, Typographer: Carl T. Herrman | Artist: Dan Cosgrove | Client: United States Postal Service

229 (2nd) Bette Davis | Design Firm: PhotoAssist, Inc., Bethesda | Art Director, Designer, Typographer: Richard Sheaff | Artist: Michael J. Deas | Client: United States Postal Service

229 (3rd) Hoover Dam Express Mail | Design Firm: PhotoAssist, Inc., Bethesda | Art Director: Carl T. Herrman | Artist: Dan Cosgrove | Designer, Typographer: Carl T. Herrman | Client: United States Postal Service

230 Living Green stamps | Design Firm: Hoyne Design, St Kilda | Creative Director: Dan Johnson | Designers: Sam Hughes, Walter Ochoa | Client: Australia Post

T-Shirts
231 Apple Store Beijing Grand Opening T-Shirt | Design Firm: Apple, Cupertino | Client: Apple

Typography
232-234 Type Faces | Design Firm: ken-tsai lee design studio, NY | Art Director, Creative Director, Design Director, Illustrator, Typographer: Ken-Tsai Lee | Designers: Ken-Tsai Lee, Chiung-Hui Chiu | Client: Harvest Ads Co., Ltd

WinnersDirectory

3 Advertising www.whois3.com
1550 Mercantile Avenue NE, Second Floor, Albuquerque, NM 87107
United States | Tel 505 293 2333 | Fax 505 293 1198

30sixty Advertising+Design, Inc. www.30sixtydesign.com
12700 Ventura Boulevard, 4th Floor, Studio City, CA 91604
United States | Tel 818 655 3100

Addison www.addison.com
20 Exchange Place, 9th Floor, New York, NY 10005, United States
Tel 212 229 5076 | Fax 212 929 3010

AG Creative www.agcreative.ca
4715 Gladstone Street, Vancouver, British Columbia v5n 5a4, Canada
Tel 604 568 0790

ALT Design www.altdesignco.com
3801 Aloha Street, Los Angeles, CA 90027, United States
Tel 323 369 1969

Alt Group www.altgroup.net
PO Box 47873, Ponsonby, Auckland 1144, New Zealand
Tel +64 9 361 4789

Ana Cortils Comunicacion Visual www.anacortils.com
Aungusto Figueroa, 32, Madrid 28004, Spain
Tel +34915224025

ANDRE GRAU
SIMSONSTRASSE 2, LEIPZIG SAXONY D-04107, Germany
Tel +49 0 341 2135 248

Apple www.apple.com
1 Infinite Loop, MS 83-PPS, Cupertino, CA 95014, United States
Tel 408 974 5286

ArthurSteenHorneAdamson www.ashawebsite.co.uk
Suite 404, Eagle Tower, Montpellier Drive, Cheltenham GL50 1TA
United Kingdom | Tel +01242 574111

The Auditorium www.christophergriffith.com
295 East 8th Street, Unit 2W, New York, NY 10009, United States
Tel 212 475 0007

Bailey Lauerman www.baileylauerman.com
1248 O Street, Suite 900, Lincoln, NE 68508, United States
Tel 402 479 0235

BBDO West www.bbdo.com
555 Market Street, 17th Floor, San Francisco, CA 94105
United States | Tel 415 808 6204

beierarbeit www.beierarbeit.de
Hobergerfeld 35, Bielefeld d 33619, Germany
Tel +49 521 7871030 | Fax +49 521 7871131

Benoit Design, Inc. www.benoitdesigninc.com
825 18th Street, Plano, TX 75074, United States
Tel 972 509 7588 | Fax 972 509 7589

Bradbury Branding & Design www.bradburydesign.com
2827 McCallum Avenue, Regina Saskatchewan S4S 0R1
Canada | Tel 306 525 4043 | Fax 306 525 4068

Breeze Creative Design Consultants www.breeze-creative.com
15 Dominie Park Balfron, Glasgow G63 0NA, United Kingdom
Tel +1360 449347 | Fax +1360 449348

Brogan & Partners www.brogan.com
325 South Old Woodward, Birmingham, MI 48009, United States
Tel 248 341 8200

Bruketa&Zinic OM www.bruketa-zinic.com
Zavrtnica 17, Zagreb 10 000, Croatia
Tel +385 1 6064 000 | Fax +385 1 6064 001

Business Architects Inc. www.b-architects.com
New Pier Takeshiba North Tower, 20F, 1-11-1, Kaigan, Minato-ku
Tokyo 105-0022, Japan | Tel +81 3 3431 2511 | Fax + 81 3 5405 4525

Cacao Design www.cacaodesign.it
18 Corso San Gottardo, Milano 20136, Italy
Tel +39 02 89422896 | Fax +39 02 58106789

CDT Design www.cdt-design.co.uk
21 Brownlow Mews, London WC1N 2LG, United Kingdom
Tel +44 207 242 0992 | Fax +44 207 242 1174

Chris van Diemen www.chrisvandiemen.com
Gildestraat 67, Delft, Zuid Holland 2624 AW, Netherlands
Tel +31 6 41920279

Clear Magazine www.clearmag.com
35710 Mound Road, Sterling Heights, MI 48310, United States
Tel 248 544 2532

Coal Creative Consultants Pte Ltd www.coal.com.sg
14B Smith Street, Singapore 58928, Singapore
Tel +65 6557 0857 | Fax +65 6557 0639

Colle + McVoy www.collemcvoy.com
400 First Avenue North, Suite 700, Minneapolis, MN 55401
United States | Tel 612 305 6000

Concrete Design Communication www.concrete.ca
2 Silver Avenue, 2nd Floor, Toronto, Ontario M6R 3A2, Canada
Tel 416 534 9960 | Fax 416 534 2184

Craig-Teerlink Design
422 Day Street, San Francisco, CA 94131-2229, United States
Tel 415 821 9591 | Fax 415 821 9591

design center ltd. www.cehovin.com
Knezova 30, Ljubljana, SI-1000, Slovenia
Tel +386 1 519 50 72

design818
Woolim Rodeosweet #414, 771-1, Janghang, Ilsan Dong, Koyang
Gyeonggi-do 410-837 Republic of Korea
Tel +82 31 902 4984

The DesignWorks Group www.thedesignworksgroup.com
PO Box 1773, Sisters, OR 97759, United States
Tel 541 549 1096 | Fax 541 549 1097

Dietwee communication and design www.dietwee.nl
Kruisdwarsstraat 2, Utrecht 3581 GL, Netherlands
Tel +31302455085 | Fax +31302333611

Direct Design www.directdesign.ru
of. 41 - 46, Zemlyanoy Val, Moscow 105064, Russian Federation
Tel +495 916 0123

Dolhem Design www.dolhemdesign.se
Nybrogatan 3, Stockholm 116 23, Sweden
Tel +08 661 50 47 | Fax +08 661 50 48

Dow Design www.dowdesign.co.nz
PO Box 8593, Symonds Street, Auckland 1150, New Zealand
Tel +64 9 303 9596

Eduardo del Fraile www.eduardodelfraile.com
Saavedra Fajardo, 7, Murcia 30001, Spain | Tel +34 968 21 18 24 | Fax +34 968 21 80 87

Elixir Design Inc. www.elixirdesign.com
2134 Van Ness Avenue, San Francisco, CA 94109, United States
Tel 415 834 0101

Emerson, Wajdowicz Studios www.designews.com
1123 Broadway, New York, NY 10010, United States
Tel 212 807 8144 | Fax 212 807 8144

Flaunt www.flaunt.com
1422 N Highland Avenue, Los Angeles, CA 90028, United States
Tel 323 836 1000 | Fax 323 856 7053

Foundry Creative www.foundrycreative.ca
1425 9th Avenue SE, Calgary, Alberta T2G0T4, Canada
Tel 403 237 8044

Frost Design www.frostdesign.com.au
1st Floor, 15 Foster Street, Surry Hills, Sydney, NSW 2026, Australia
Tel +61 2 9280 4233 | Fax +0061 2 9280 4266

Goodby, Silverstein & Partners www.goodbysilverstein.com
720 California Street, San Francisco, CA 94108, United States
Tel 415 955 5683

GQ www.condenast.com
4 Times Square Plaza, 9th Floor, New York, NY 10036, United States
Tel 212 286 6696 | Fax 212 286 8515

The Halo Group www.thehalogroup.net
350 7th Avenue, 21st Floor, New York, NY 10001, United States
Tel 212 643 9700 | Fax 212 871 0150

Hartford Design www.hartfordesign.com
651 W. Washington, Suite 503, Chicago, IL 60661, United States
Tel 312 756 5600

HL2 www.hl2.com
222 Dexter Avenue N, Seattle, WA 98109, United States | Tel 206 223-0055

Hornall Anderson www.hornallanderson.com
710 2nd Avenue, Suite 1300, Seattle, WA 98104, United States
Tel 206 826 2329 | Fax 206 467 6411

Hoyne Design www.hoyne.com.au
Level 1, 77a Acland Street, St Kilda, Victoria 3182, Australia
Tel +03 9537 182

IMAGE: Global Vision www.imageglobalvision.com
2525 Main Street, Suite 204, Santa Monica, CA 90405, United States
Tel 310 998 8898 | Fax 310 396 1686

JB Design www.jberrydesign.com
23 Newfield Street, Norwalk, CT 06850, United States
Tel 203 750 9698

Jessica Campbell www.more-than-skin-deep.com
4750 N Clarendon Avenue, Apt 1001, Chicago, IL 60640
United States | Tel 585 739 9136

Jill Greenberg Studio www.manipulator.com
8570 Wilshire Boulevard, Suite 250, Beverly Hills, CA 90211
United States | Tel 310 360 6260 | Fax 310 360 6202

Jones Worldwide www.jonesingfor.com
720 N. Franklin, Suite 401, Chicago, IL 60610, United States
Tel 312 266 6100

Karen Lukas-Hardy Design
3776 Turnberry Court, Duluth, GA 30096, United States | Tel 678 473 9844

Kellerhouse, Inc. www.kellerhouse.com
2737 Vista Del Mar Road, Topanga, CA 90290, United States
Tel 310 455 2684

Ken-Tsai Lee Design Studio www.kentsailee.com
99-44 62nd Road, Rego Park, New York, NY 11374, United States
Tel 718 699 6585

Kibrit & Calce www.kibritecalce.it
Via Cardassi, 66, Bari 70121, Italy | Tel +39 080 5589033 | Fax +39 080 5978854

KNOCK Inc. www.knockinc.com
219 North Second Street, Suite 404, Minneapolis, MN 55401
United States | Tel 612 333 6511 | Fax 612 455 6866

L&C Design Studio
10F. No.31-1, Lane 225, Sec. 2, Wunhua Road, Banciao 220
Taiwan, Province Of China | Tel +8860958905343

Landor Associates, San Francisco www.landor.com
1001 Front Street, San Francisco, CA 94111, United States
Tel 415 365 3679 | Fax 415 365 3197

Landor Associates, Sydney www.landor.com
Level 11, 15 Blue Street, North Sydney, New South Wales 2060
Australia | Tel +61 2 8908 8703

Lloyd & Company Advertising, Inc. www.lloydandco.com
180 Varick Street, Suite 1018, New York, NY 10014, United States
Tel 212 414 3100 | Fax 212 414 3113

Lorenc+Yoo Design www.lorencyoodesign.com
109 Vickery Street, Roswell, GA 30075, United States
Tel 770 645 2828 | Fax 770 998 2452

LOWERCASE, INC. www.lowercaseinc.com
213 West Institute Place, Suite 311, Chicago, IL 60610, United States
Tel 312 274 0659

MacLaren McCann, Calgary www.maclaren.com
238 11 Avenue SE, Calgary, Alberta T2G 0X8, Canada | Tel 403 261 7155

Manarchy Films www.manarchy.com
656 W. Hubbard Street, Chicago, IL 60654, United States
Tel 312 666 7400 | Fax 312 666 2400

Matsumoto Inc. www.matsumotoinc.com
127 West 26th Street, Suite 900, New York, NY 10001, United States
Tel 212 807 0248 | Fax 212 807 1527

Melissa Collins | Graphic Design
Longford Station, Bendemeer, NSW 2355, Australia
Tel +61 2 6769 6728 | Fax +61 2 6769 6516

Methodologie www.methodologie.com
720 Third Avenue, Suite 800, Seattle, WA 98104-1870, United States
Tel 206 623 1044 | Fax 206 625 0154

Michael Osborne Design www.modsf.com
444 De Haro Street, Suite 207, San Francisco, CA 94107, United States
Tel 415 255 0125 | Fax 415 255 1312

Michael Schwab Studio www.michaelschwab.com
108 Tamalpais Avenue, San Anselmo, CA 94960, United States
Tel 415 257 5792

MiresBall www.miresball.com
2345 Kettner Boulevard, San Diego, CA 92101, United States
Tel 619 234 6631

Mirko Ilic Corp www.mirkoilic.com
207 E 32nd Street, 4th Floor, New York, NY 10016, United States
Tel 212 481 9737 | Fax 212 481 7088

MIYAGRAPHIX
PinessPlaza, 2-103, 2-25-14, Kichijojiminamicho,
Musashinoshi, Tokyo 180-0003, Japan
Tel +81 422 46 2938 | Fax +81 422 46 2938

Modulation Design www.modulationdesign.com
35 New Road, Kendall Park, NJ 08824, United States
Tel 908-208-4384

Monahan & Rhee www.monahan-rhee.com
403 Broome Street, New York, NY 10013, United States
Tel 212 925 9202 | Fax 212 925 9207

North Charles Street Design Organization www.ncsdo.com
222 West Saratoga Street, Baltimore, MD 21201-3512
United States | Tel 410 539 4040 | Fax 410 685 0961

Novita Communications www.novitapr.com
222A 6th Avenue, Brooklyn, NY 11215, United States
Tel 718 783 3160 | Fax 718 398 2591

Office www.visitoffice.com
1060 Capp Street, San Francisco, CA 94115, United States
Tel 415 447 9850 | Fax 415 447 9208

OLSON www.oco.com
1625 Hennepin Avenue, Minneapolis, MN 55403, United States
Tel 612 215 9800 | Fax 612 215 9801

Ontwerphaven www.ontwerphaven.nl
Noordstraat 83, Tilburg 5038 EH, Netherlands
Tel +06 50804098

The Partners www.thepartners.co.uk
Albion Courtyard, Greenhill Rents, Smithfield, London EC1M 6PQ
United Kingdom | Tel +20 7689 4618

Penguin Graphics
5-12-24-102 Ushitahonmachi, Higashi-ku Hiroshima 732-0066
Japan | Tel +81 82 511 1371 | Fax +81 82 511 1372

PENGUIN GROUP (USA) INC. www.us.penguingroup.com
375 Hudson Street, 3rd Floor, New York, NY 10014, United States
Tel 212 366 2372

Pentagram Design, Austin www.pentagram.com
1508 West Fifth Street, Austin, TX 78703, United States
Tel 512 476 3076 | Fax 512 476 5725

Pentagram Design, Berlin www.pentagram.com
Leibnizstrasse 60, Berlin 10629, Germany
Tel +49 30 27 87 610 | Fax +49 30 27 87 61 10

Pentagram Design, New York www.pentagram.com
204 Fifth Avenue, New York, NY 10010, United States
Tel 212 683 7000 | Fax 212 532 0181

Pentagram Design, San Francisco www.pentagram.com
387 Tehama Street, San Francisco, CA 94103, United States
Tel 415 896 0499 | Fax 415 896 0555

Peter Kraemer www.peterkraemer-web.de
Lindemannstr. 31, Düsseldorf 40237, Germany
Tel +211 210 80 87 | Fax +211 22 85 41

Peter Mendelsund Design www.mendelsund.com
1745 Broadway, 19th Floor, New York, NY 10019, United States
Tel 212 572 2217

Peterson Ray & Company www.peterson.com
311 N. Market Street, Suite 311, Dallas, TX 75202, United States
Tel 214 954 0522 | Fax 214 954 1161

PhilippeBecker www.beckersf.com
612 Howard Street, Suite 200, San Francisco, CA 94105, United States
Tel 415 348 0054 | Fax 415 348 0063

PhotoAssist, Inc. www.photoassist.com
7735 Old Georgetown Road, Lower Level, Bethesda, MD 20814
United States | Tel 240 644 1941

Poulin + Morris Inc. www.poulinmorris.com
286 Spring Street, Sixth Floor, New York, NY 10013, United States
Tel 212 675 1332

Punktum Design MDD www.punktumdesign.dk
Pakhus 12, Dampfaergevej 8-5th Floor, Copenhagen, DK 2100
Denmark | Tel +45 20320063

Rebeca Méndez Design www.rebecamendez.com
11009 1/2 Strathmore Drive, Los Angeles, CA 90024, United States
Tel 310 985 0621

René Milot Illustations Inc. www.renemilot.com
49 Thorncliffe Park Drive, Suite 1604, Toronto, Ontario M4H 1J6
Canada | Tel 416 425 7726 | Fax 416 707 7665

Rob Duncan Design www.robduncandesign.com
2 Townsend Street, Apt 1-503, San Francisco, CA 94107, United States
Tel 415 706 7869

Ron Taft Design www.rontaft.com
PMB 372, 2934 Beverly Glen Circle, Los Angeles, CA 90077
United States | Tel 310 472 7193

Saatchi Design Worldwide www.saatchi.com
PO Box 801, Auckland, New Zealand
Tel +64 9 355 5000 | Fax +64 9 355 1838

Sage Brandworks www.sagebrandworks.com
3176 Camino Colorados, Lafayette, CA 94549, United States
Tel 925 299 1540 | Fax 925 299 1546

Sense Team www.sensebrand.com
15C Block B, City of Garden, Jintang Road, Shenzhen, China
Tel 510 549 1405

Sibley/Peteet Design www.spdaustin.com
522 East 6th, Austin, TX 78701, United States | Tel 512 473 2333

Siegel+Gale www.siegelgale.com
625 Avenue of the Americas, 4th Floor, New York, NY 10011
United States | Tel 212 453 0400 | Fax 212 453 0401

Squires & Company www.squirescompany.com
2913 Canton Street, Dallas, TX 75226, United States
Tel 214 939 9194 | Fax 214 939 3464

St. Martin's Press us.macmillan.com/smp.aspx
75 Fifth Avenue, Suite 401, New York, NY 10010, United States
Tel 646 307 5100 | Fax 212 529 1540

Strømme Throndsen Design www.stdesign.no
Holtegata 22, 0355 Oslo, Norway | Tel +47 22 96 39 00

Studio International www.studio-international.com
Buconjiceva 43, Zagreb HR-10 000, Croatia (local Name: Hrvatska)
Tel +385 1 37 40 404 | Fax +385 1 37 08 320

Studio Joseph Jibri www.josephjibri.com
20 Wissotzky Street, Tel Aviv 62338, Israel | Tel +972 3 6850037 | Fax +972 3 5443614

Studio Rasic www.studio-rasic.hr
Meduliceva 1, Zagreb 10000, Croatia | Tel +385 1 4847 224

Subplot Design Inc. www.subplot.com
301-318 Homer Street, Vancouver, British Columbia V6B 2V2, Canada
Tel 604 685 2990 | Fax 604 685 2909

Tank Design Inc. www.tankdesign.com
158 Sidney Street, Cambridge, MA 02139, United States
Tel 617 995 4000 | Fax 617 995 4001

TAXI CANADA Inc. www.taxi.ca
495 Wellington Street West, Suite 102, Totonto, Ontario M5V 1E9
Canada | Tel 416 979 7001 | Fax 416 979 7626

tbd advertising www.tbdadvertising.com
856 NW Bond Street, Suite 2, Bend, OR 97701, United States
Tel 541 388 7558 | Fax 541 388 7532

TOKY Branding + Design www.toky.com
3001 Locust Street, St. Louis, MO 63103, United States
Tel 314 534 2000 | Fax 314 534 2001

Tomorrow Partners www.tomorrowpartners.com
2332 5th Street, Berkeley, CA 94710, United States | Tel 510 644 2332

TompertDesign www.tompertdesign.com
216 Fulton Street, Palo Alto, CA 94301, United States
Tel 650 323 0365

Turner Duckworth www.turnerduckworth.com
831 Montgomery Street, San Francisco, CA 94133, United States
Tel 415 675 7777

Underline Studio www.underlinestudio.com
26 Soho Street, Suite 204, Toronto, Ontario M5V 1Z7, Canada
Tel 416 341-0475

UNIT Design Collective www.unitcollective.com
1416 Larkin Street, Unit B, San Francisco, CA 94109, United States
Tel 415 409 0000 | Fax 503 210 1395

Vanderbyl Design www.vanderbyldesign.com
171 2nd Street, 2nd Floor, San Francisco, CA 94105, United States
Tel 415 543 8447 | Fax 415 543 9058

Venables Bell & Partners www.venablesbell.com
201 Post Street, Suite 200, San Francisco, CA 94111, United States
Tel 415 962 3067

Visual Arts Press, Ltd.
www.schoolofvisualarts.edu/publishing/index.jsp?sid0=81&sid1=82
220 East 23 Street, Suite 311, New York, NY 10010, United States
Tel 212 592 2380 | Fax 212 696 0552

Visual Voice www.vslvc.net
706 N. Oak Park, Oak Park, IL 60302, United States | Tel 312 480 1183

Visualink Creative www.vlcreative.com
256 Seaboard Lane, Suite A-101, Franklin, TN 37067, United States
Tel 615 771 0500 | Fax 615 771 0505

Volume Inc. www.volumesf.com
2130 Harrison Street, Suite B, San Francisco, CA 94110, United States
Tel 415 503 0800 | Fax 415 503 0818

VSA Partners, New York www.vsapartners.com
268 West 44th Street, New York, NY 10036, United States
Tel 212 869 1188 | Fax 212 869 0099

WAX www.waxpartnership.com
320 333 24th Avenue SW, Calgary, Alberta T2T 0J5, Canada
Tel 403 262 9323 | Fax 403 626 9399

Webster Design Associates www.websterdesign.com
5060 Dodge Street, Suite 2000, Omaha, NE 68132, United States
Tel 402 551 1410

WONGDOODY www.wongdoody.com
1011 Western Avenue, Suite 900, Seattle, WA 98104, United States
Tel 206 624 5325 | Fax 206 624 2369

Y&L / 2nd Globe www.yandl.com
407 Fulton Street, Indianapolis, IN 46202, United States
Tel 317 264 8000 | Fax 317 264 8001

Young & Laramore www.yandl.com
407 Fulton Street, Indianapolis, IN 46202, United States
Tel 317 264 8000 | Fax 317 264 8001

DesignFirms

Clients

Two ways to dramatically save on our Books!

Book Subscriptions (Standing Orders):
50% off or $35 for a $70 book, plus $10 for shipping & handling
Get our new books at our best deal, long before they arrive in book
stores! A Standing Order is a subscription commiment to the Graphis
books of your choice.

Pre-Publication Sales:
35% off or $45 for a $70 book, plus $10 for shipping & handling
Our next best deal. Sign-up today at www.graphis.com to receive our
pre-publication sale invitations! Order early and save!

Graphis Design Titles

Poster Annual 2010

Design Annual 2009

New Talent Annual 2009

Advertising 2010

Annual Reports 2009

Brochures 6

Letterhead 7

Logo 7

Product Design 3

Promotion Design 2

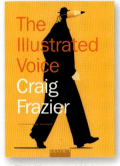
The Illustrated Voice

12 Japanese Masters

designing:
Chermayeff & Geismar

Exhibition:
The Work of Socio X

Masters 20th Century

Please visit www.graphis.com for more information on each title.